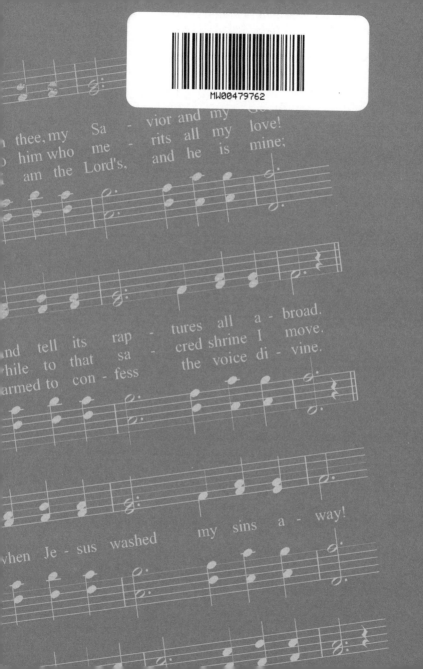

Oh happy day

SOUL-STIRRING INSPIRATIONS
WITH A GOSPEL MUSIC TWIST

KEN PETERSEN

Tyndale House Publishers
Carol Stream, Illinois

LIVING EXPRESSIONS

COLLECTION

Living Expressions invites you to explore God's Word in a way that is refreshing to your spirit and restorative to your soul.

Visit Tyndale online at tyndale.com.

TYNDALE, Tyndale's quill logo, *Living Expressions*, and the Living Expressions logo are registered trademarks of Tyndale House Ministries.

Oh Happy Day: Soul-Stirring Inspirations with a Gospel Music Twist

Designed by Ron C. Kaufmann

For information about special discounts for bulk purchases, please contact Tyndale House Publishers at csresponse@tyndale.com, or call 1-800-323-9400.

ISBN 978-1-4964-4639-8

Printed in China

27   26   25   24   23   22   21
7   6   5   4   3   2   1

Contents

MAKE A JOYFUL NOISE UNTO THE LORD, ALL YE LANDS.

SERVE THE LORD WITH GLADNESS:

COME BEFORE HIS PRESENCE WITH SINGING.

PSALM 100:1-2, KJV

Amazing Grace

We've sung this beloved hymn at events ranging from festivals to funerals. The lyrics encapsulate John Newton's life story. Forced into service on a British merchant ship when he was eighteen, Newton eventually found himself in West Africa, sick with malaria and suffering mistreatment from others. On the trip home, the ship nearly sank during a violent storm, but miraculously, the crew survived. Newton realized God had intervened, and his life was changed forever. The Lord's "rich mercy . . . preserved, restored, [and] pardoned" him, words inscribed on his gravestone. How about you? Take a moment to let God know how precious his grace is to you.

Father God, I have not forgotten that you rescued me from a life of despair and self-destruction. Thank you for loving me unconditionally and being merciful to me.

BY GRACE ARE YE SAVED THROUGH FAITH; AND THAT NOT OF YOURSELVES: IT IS THE GIFT OF GOD: NOT OF WORKS, LEST ANY MAN SHOULD BOAST.

EPHESIANS 2:8-9, KJV

John Newton's spiritual growth was gradual; he continued to be a slave trader for six years after his life-changing experience. In 1764, he was ordained by the Church of England. In 1788, Newton wrote a graphic account of the slave trade to support the antislavery movement. Newton lived to see the slave trade abolished in Britain.

Boundless Love

One line in this catchy gospel song describes how Jesus wants to love us because we are precious to him. We are treasured by the Son of God, and he longs to lavish his love upon us. That's pretty mind-boggling, isn't it? And yet sometimes we block that intimate relationship. Why would we resist the love of God? It could be that we have been hurt before. Possibly we're afraid of what responding to the love of Jesus might require. Maybe we have idols and sins in our lives that we aren't willing to let go of. What is keeping you from receiving God's boundless love?

Jesus, I know you want to love me, but I have been pushing you away. Help me to let your love pour in by breaking down the walls I've built in my heart.

I AM PERSUADED, THAT NEITHER DEATH, NOR LIFE, NOR ANGELS, NOR PRINCIPALITIES, NOR POWERS, NOR THINGS PRESENT, NOR THINGS TO COME, NOR HEIGHT, NOR DEPTH, NOR ANY OTHER CREATURE, SHALL BE ABLE TO SEPARATE US FROM THE LOVE OF GOD, WHICH IS IN CHRIST JESUS OUR LORD.
ROMANS 8:38-39, KJV

Dianne Wilkinson has written more than a thousand gospel songs and has had many number one hits between the Southern Gospel and Bluegrass Gospel charts. For two decades she worked closely with The Cathedrals, the legendary quartet whose knee-slapping version of "Boundless Love" at a reunion concert is Southern Gospel at its best.

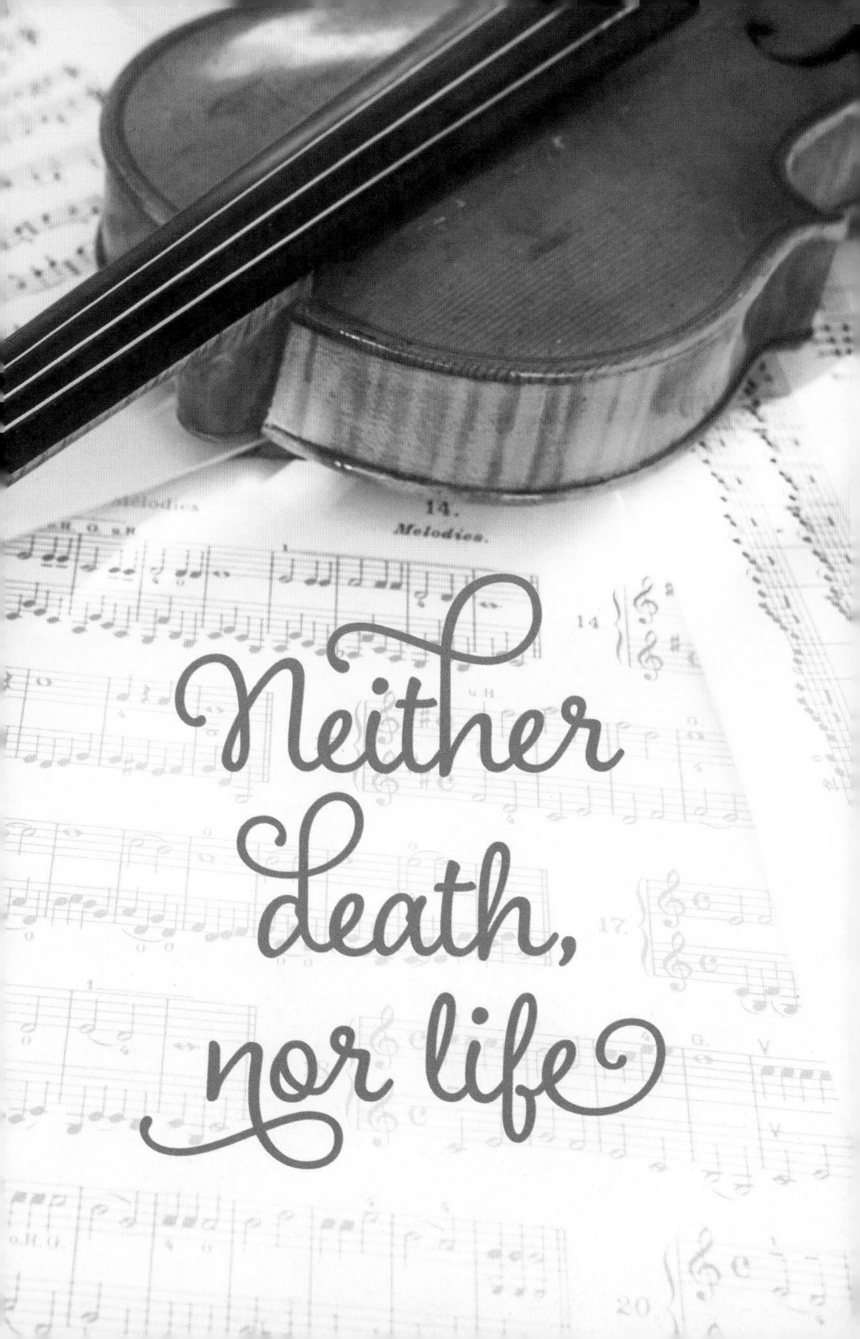

Neither death, nor life

The offering for our sin

What a Savior

Southern Gospel music is filled with deep awe and gratitude for Jesus' sacrifice on the cross, which saves us from eternal separation from God. When Ernie Haase and Signature Sound sing this favorite, their joy is undeniable. It's evident they cannot wait to sing for their Savior when they see him face-to-face. And yet it's easy to hear the salvation message so many times that we start to take it for granted. Revisit Calvary and meditate on the extraordinary act of redemption that changed the world forever. Jesus died because he loves you. Let his love flood your heart.

Lord God, I need a personal revival. Help me reclaim my original passion for you. Jesus, I can't thank you enough for saving me from my sins.

GOD MADE CHRIST, WHO NEVER SINNED, TO BE THE OFFERING FOR OUR SIN, SO THAT WE COULD BE MADE RIGHT WITH GOD THROUGH CHRIST.
2 CORINTHIANS 5:21

Marvin P. Dalton's songs were often included at camp meetings in the 1940s and 50s. One of his other popular tunes was "Looking for a City." For a time, Dalton was a member of the famed Hartford Quartet, which in its history featured a number of Southern Gospel artists and songwriters.

Alabama Mud

Through the lyrics of this song, Belinda Smith transports us to a muddy riverbank at an old-fashioned baptism. The power of the moment comes alive in her description. Your own baptism may not have taken place in a river; people are immersed in oceans, swimming pools, and even bathtubs, all with witnesses standing by. Since Jesus was surrounded by others when John the Baptist performed his baptism, we follow that example. Baptism symbolizes that when you died to sin, you were given "a new heart . . . a new spirit" (Ezekiel 36:26). May these precious gifts continually reflect God's presence in your life.

Jesus, when you saved me, I wanted to be baptized. I died to my old self and was raised to new life in you. I am not ashamed to be your follower.

WE DIED AND WERE BURIED WITH CHRIST BY BAPTISM. AND JUST AS CHRIST WAS RAISED FROM THE DEAD BY THE GLORIOUS POWER OF THE FATHER, NOW WE ALSO MAY LIVE NEW LIVES.

ROMANS 6:4

Belinda Smith is a performer and songwriter who shares her gifts by mentoring up-and-coming musical talent. She has been a featured artist at Nashville's Bluebird Cafe. Her collaborative song with Cindi Ballard and Wayne Haun, "So Many Years, So Many Blessings," performed by The Lewis Family, won the 2004 Dove Award for Bluegrass Song of the Year.

Live new lives

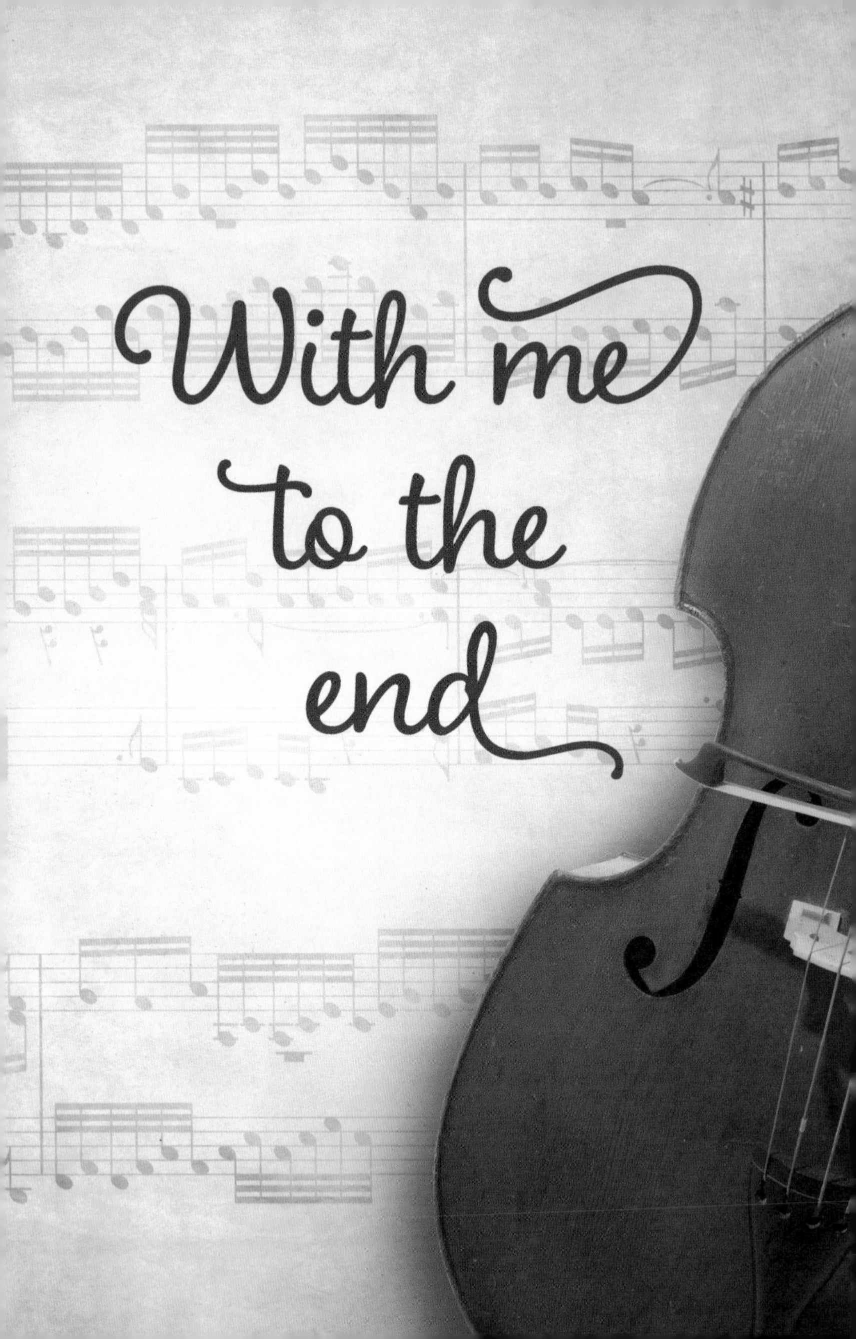
With me
to the
end

'Tis So Sweet to Trust in Jesus

Susan and Austin Whisnant and Jim Brady gave a heartfelt performance of this hymn during a Gospel Music Hymn Sing. God is in control, but are you okay with that? It's easy to say we trust God when things are going well. But when life becomes difficult, we may question, worry, and begin to doubt God's love. Remember, he never promised us a carefree life, but he did promise to never abandon those who search for him (Psalm 9:10). Welcome each day with complete confidence in God. Trust him so deeply that you can sing his praises, no matter what happens.

God, I come to you confessing my lack of faith. Bolster my reliance on you.
Help me to trust you fully and completely, no matter what life brings me.

THE LORD IS MY STRENGTH AND MY SHIELD; MY HEART
TRUSTS IN HIM, AND HE HELPS ME. MY HEART LEAPS FOR JOY,
AND WITH MY SONG I PRAISE HIM.

PSALM 28:7, NIV

Louisa M. R. Stead was enjoying the beach with her family when cries for help changed their lives. Louisa's husband rushed into the water to save a drowning boy, and both perished after he was pulled under. Shortly following that traumatic incident, Jesus' sweet presence consoled Louisa as she wrote this song from her heart.

How Great Thou Art

Originating in Sweden in 1885 as a poem by Carl Boberg, "How Great Thou Art" has become one of the most recorded gospel songs ever. The lyrics describe the mightiness of God, and the circuitous journey to its present form also testifies of God's mighty hand. If not for George Beverly Shea's sense of its enduring message, leading him to sing it at a 1955 Billy Graham Crusade, the song might not have been heard around the world. In 1957, Shea sang it ninety-nine times during an extended New York Crusade. Right now, let your voice soar in praise as you, too, sing this great hymn.

God and Father of all, I humbly come to you. I can't fully grasp how mighty you are. But I am thankful for your presence in my life.

EVER SINCE THE WORLD WAS CREATED, PEOPLE HAVE SEEN THE EARTH AND SKY. THROUGH EVERYTHING GOD MADE, THEY CAN CLEARLY SEE HIS INVISIBLE QUALITIES—HIS ETERNAL POWER AND DIVINE NATURE.

ROMANS 1:20

Missionary and linguist Stuart Hine learned of the Russian version of Boberg's poem and in 1949 translated it into English and added new verses. According to Manna Music, there are more than 1,700 documented recordings of this song, from George Beverly Shea to Elvis Presley to Carrie Underwood, and hundreds in between.

His
eternal
power
and divine
nature

He Set Me Free

There's a popular T-shirt with a familiar Southernism: "Raised on Sweet Tea and Liberty." Does that describe your life right now? Or do you feel shackled by sin? Maybe you don't even recognize how imprisoned you are. But God knows. He "spread[s] out our sins . . . our secret sins" (Psalm 90:8). And yet, he wants to set us free from the "power of darkness" (Colossians 1:13, KJV). God is more powerful than Satan. Won't you confess your sins and allow his loving mercy to set you on a light-filled path? Then you can replace that T-shirt with another one: "Raised on Sweet Tea and *Jesus*."

> *Lord Jesus, I am trapped in a cage of my own making,*
> *weighed down by my sins. I know you hold the key to release me.*
> *Thank you for your mercy and grace.*

WHO WILL FREE ME FROM THIS LIFE THAT IS DOMINATED BY SIN AND DEATH? THANK GOD! THE ANSWER IS IN JESUS CHRIST OUR LORD.

ROMANS 7:24-25

Albert Brumley learned his songwriting skills from E. M. Bartlett at the Hartford Music Institute. After graduating, Brumley worked for Bartlett making songbooks and teaching in the traveling Singing School. Song ideas kept coming. "He Set Me Free" was published in 1939.

What a Lovely Name

When Vestal Goodman sang this song about the wonders of Jesus, her powerful voice soared as she celebrated the power of his name. The lovely name of Jesus is also known by other names and descriptions—Lord, Redeemer, Shepherd, King, Bread of Life, Lamb of God. There are hundreds of them. In the spirit of this well-loved song, here's an idea to consider: Look up the biblical names attributed to Jesus, and write down the ten that mean the most to you. Each day, pull out your list, select one name, and thank Jesus for its personal significance.

Lord Jesus, you are the Light of the World, my Advocate, my Savior.
Show me all the ways you embody the attributes of your name.
Help me to always honor your name.

GOD ALSO HATH HIGHLY EXALTED HIM, AND GIVEN HIM A NAME
WHICH IS ABOVE EVERY NAME: THAT AT THE NAME OF JESUS EVERY KNEE
SHOULD BOW . . . AND THAT EVERY TONGUE SHOULD CONFESS
THAT JESUS CHRIST IS LORD.
PHILIPPIANS 2:9-11, KJV

Charles B. Wycuff was introduced to gospel singing conventions in Alabama at a young age, since his father sang in a local quartet. Wycuff's songwriting path was set. He wrote this Southern Gospel classic in 1967, using his gift of creating songs to share God's love with the world.

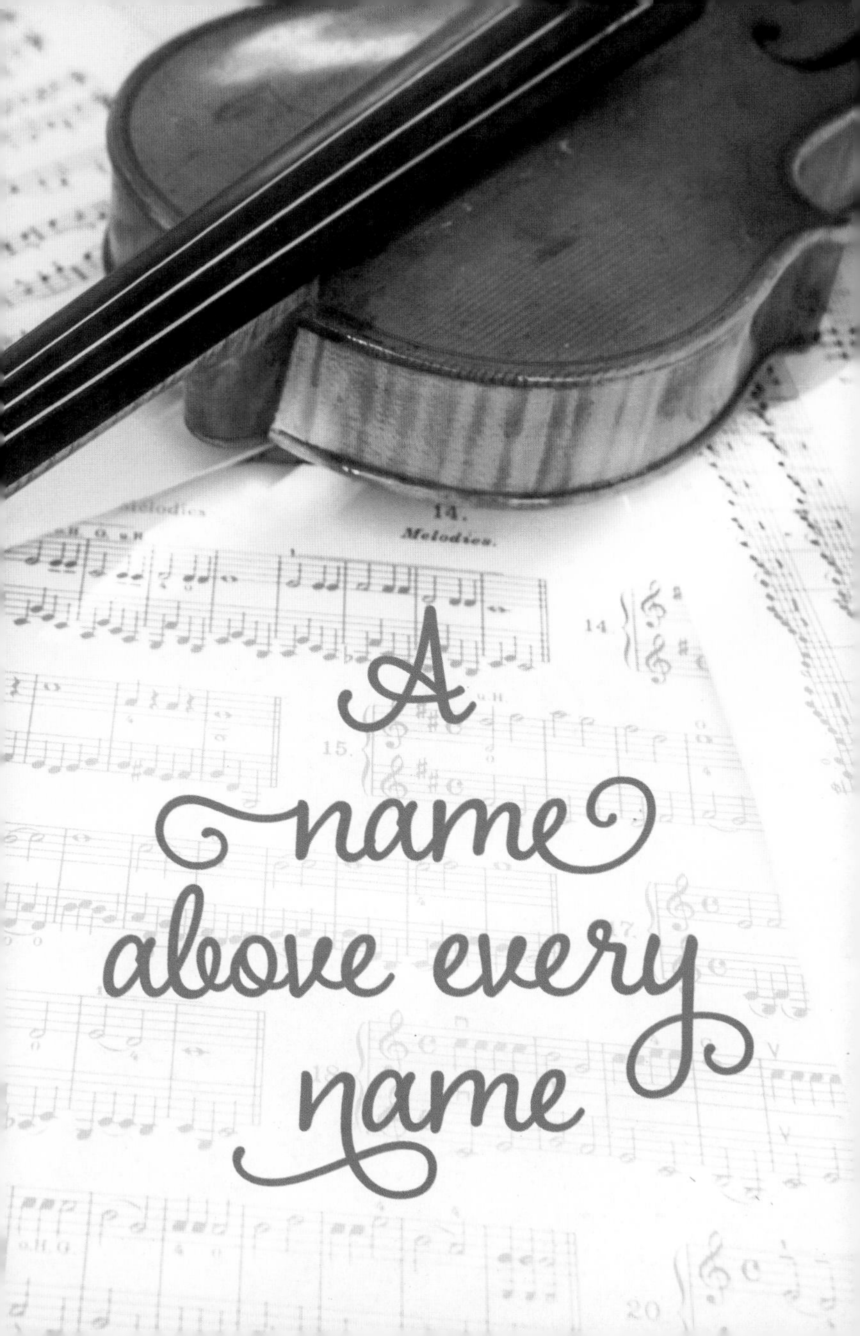
A name above every name
14.
Melodies.

Sweet, Sweet Spirit

How has the Holy Spirit been working in your life lately? Has he been whispering in your ear? How are you responding to him? Sometimes we are so loud and talkative that we don't hear his voice. "Sweet, Sweet Spirit" is a song a worship leader might ask his congregation to sing quietly as a way of inviting the Holy Spirit into their midst. Maybe you could consider singing it prayerfully each day before you come before the Lord, before you close your mouth and just listen. Open yourself to God's Spirit, and let him work in your life today.

Dear God, I have experienced your Spirit many times,
but I want more of him. Help me to be aware of the Spirit's promptings
and to respond to your guidance and direction.

THE COMFORTER, WHICH IS THE HOLY GHOST, WHOM THE FATHER WILL
SEND IN MY NAME, HE SHALL TEACH YOU ALL THINGS.

JOHN 14:26, KJV

African American gospel songwriter Doris Mae Akers started playing piano when she was six years old. In 1958, Akers formed the Sky Pilot Choir, the first interracial choir in Los Angeles. The Smithsonian honored her songs and recordings as national treasures. In 2011, she was inducted into the Southern Gospel Music Association Hall of Fame.

He Touched Me

Jesus' act was audacious—he put his hand on a leper to heal him. The Son of God broke religious and social taboos to physically touch a sick man. In a time when pandemics are all too real, the meaning is no longer lost: Because of sin, we are all lepers; we are all carriers; we are all diseased. And yet Jesus extends his hand to each one of us. He reaches across time and space to ease the hurt, shame, and agony you bear. Whatever circumstances you're in right now, receive his precious healing touch.

*Jesus, I need your healing hand to take away the disease
of sin that plagues me. Please restore my spirit and give me
strength to battle Satan's temptations.*

A MAN WITH LEPROSY CAME AND KNELT IN FRONT OF JESUS, BEGGING TO BE
HEALED. "IF YOU ARE WILLING, YOU CAN HEAL ME AND MAKE ME CLEAN,"
HE SAID. MOVED WITH COMPASSION, JESUS REACHED OUT AND TOUCHED
HIM. "I AM WILLING," HE SAID. "BE HEALED!" INSTANTLY THE LEPROSY
DISAPPEARED, AND THE MAN WAS HEALED.

MARK 1:40-42

Bill and Gloria Gaither's contributions to gospel music have earned the couple countless awards and accolades. "He Touched Me" was written by Bill in 1963 and recorded twice within four years by The Imperials. Elvis Presley heard their 1969 version and used the group as backup singers for his 1971 recording.

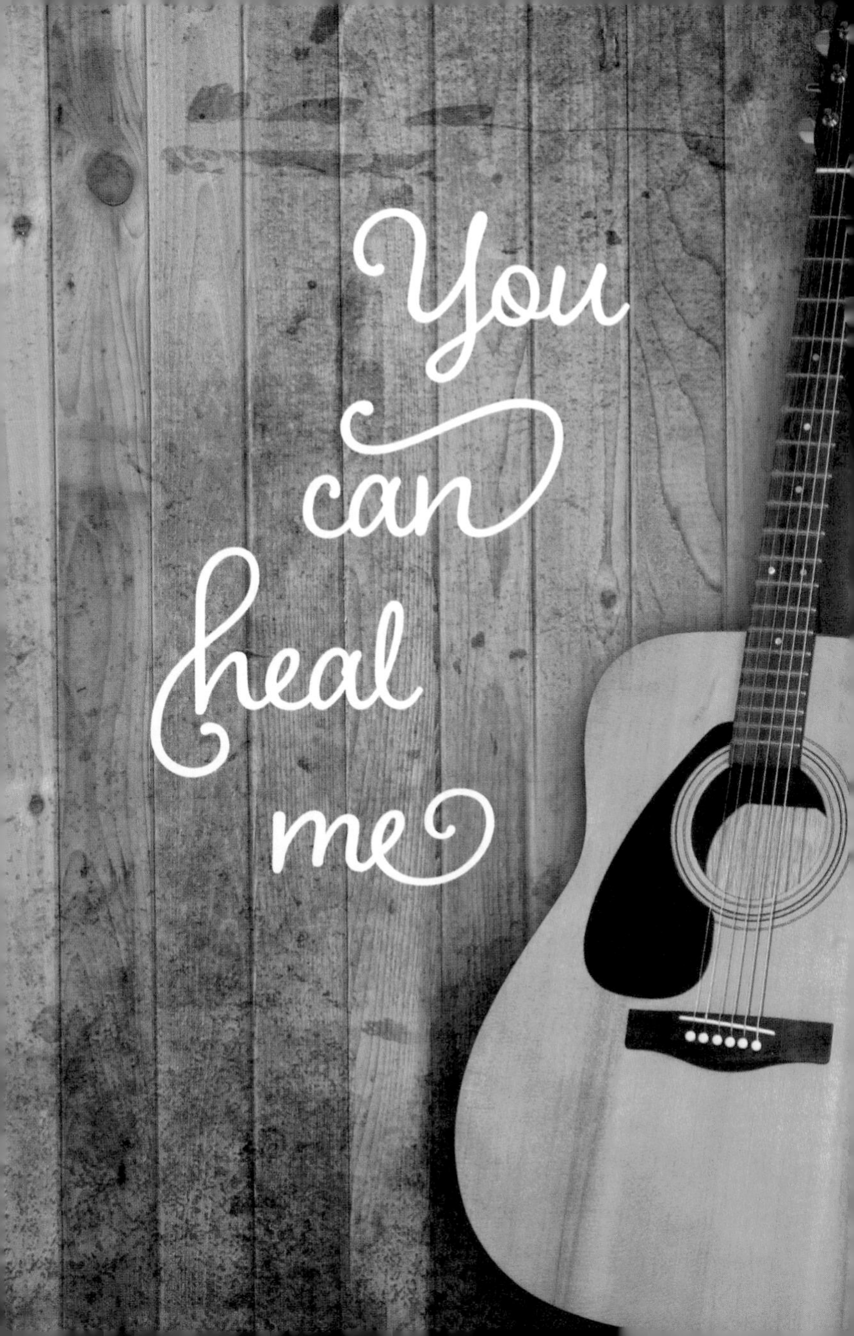
You can heal me

New birth and new life

Oh Happy Day

It might surprise you that the foundation of the 1969 hit song "Oh Happy Day," by the Edwin Hawkins Singers, was a hymn refrain written in the 1700s. Yes, the message of an old hymn rings true more than two centuries later, even when it's wrapped in a modern gospel sound. Why not make this the truth you celebrate today? Maybe doing this is a good way to sweep your troubles away and focus on the most important thing of all. Rejoice because of what Jesus did for you. Embrace it, sing it, and live it. Oh happy day, indeed!

Lord, thank you for cleansing me from sin, for making me your child,
and for promising me eternal life with you.

WHEN GOD OUR SAVIOR REVEALED HIS KINDNESS AND LOVE, HE SAVED US, NOT BECAUSE OF THE RIGHTEOUS THINGS WE HAD DONE, BUT BECAUSE OF HIS MERCY. HE WASHED AWAY OUR SINS, GIVING US A NEW BIRTH AND NEW LIFE THROUGH THE HOLY SPIRIT.

TITUS 3:4-5

Philip Doddridge was a pastor and hymn writer in eighteenth-century England. He wrote more than four hundred hymns that were published after his death. Edwin Hawkins was a gospel musician, choir director, and composer who won his first Grammy with this song. When "Oh Happy Day" made the pop charts, sales hit seven million copies.

Jesus Is Coming Soon

While many Southern Gospel songs address life's troubles and how God provides power to prevail, just as many lyrics highlight the excitement of Jesus' return. In light of this wondrous event, how are you living now? Does believing that Jesus will come again make a difference in what you say and do, how urgently you share the good news of salvation with loved ones and friends? The Bible says we won't know when the Second Coming will happen, but imagine if it were *today*. How would you conduct yourself differently in the hours before his arrival?

> *Lord Jesus, I admit my attention tends to focus on my current circumstances and not your return. Even though I don't know when it will happen, help me be ready.*

I WILL COME AGAIN, AND RECEIVE YOU UNTO MYSELF; THAT WHERE I AM, THERE YE MAY BE ALSO.

JOHN 14:3, KJV

R. E. Winsett wrote more than a thousand gospel songs and was an important songbook publisher in the early twentieth century. "Jesus Is Coming Soon" won Gospel Song of the Year at the 1969 Dove Awards. Winsett was inducted into both the Southern Gospel Music Association Hall of Fame and the Gospel Music Hall of Fame.

So dear to my childhood

The Church in the Wildwood

In 1854, a music teacher named William Pitts took a stagecoach from Wisconsin to Iowa to visit his fiancée. During a rest stop in Iowa, Pitts found a wooded lot that seemed perfect for a country church. Returning home, he couldn't get that idea out of his head and wrote a poem that would become the song. Like many Southern Gospel songs, "The Church in the Wildwood" longs for the past. But maybe it's more than just sentimental; maybe it's also a pull inviting listeners into sweet fellowship with God. After all, he promises to be there in your midst.

Dear God, I yearn for the nostalgic times this song represents.
Please give me a simple faith and a strong commitment to my own church.
I treasure your sweet presence when we all meet together.

DRAW NIGH TO GOD, AND HE WILL DRAW NIGH TO YOU.

JAMES 4:8, KJV

The residents of Bradford, Iowa, were unaware of William Pitts and the poem that would become the song when they built a church on the exact spot he had envisioned one. It was completed in 1864, and Pitts introduced his song at the dedication. The Little Brown Church continues to be an active Congregational church.

I Love to Tell the Story

When gospel artist Mark Lowry performs this song, you hear how personal the words are to him. That heartfelt connection conveys a lot. The Bible is not only the story of God and his Son, Jesus, but also the story of each of us as well. Think about it: the story of *Jesus and you*. As the lyrics say, Jesus satisfies your longings, "as nothing else can do." How is that true in your life? Take time right now to reflect on how the "old, old story" of Jesus has made your life into a "new, new song."

Lord, you know my story better than anyone else. Thank you for all you have done for me. Please give me opportunities to boldly share your truth.

THAT WHICH WE HAVE SEEN AND HEARD WE DECLARE TO YOU, THAT YOU ALSO MAY HAVE FELLOWSHIP WITH US; AND TRULY OUR FELLOWSHIP IS WITH THE FATHER AND WITH HIS SON JESUS CHRIST.

1 JOHN 1:3, NKJV

During a severe illness, hymn writer Catherine Hankey was compelled to compose a long poem about Jesus. The first portion became "Tell Me the Old, Old Story," while the rest of the lines became the basis for "I Love to Tell the Story."

Jesus and his love

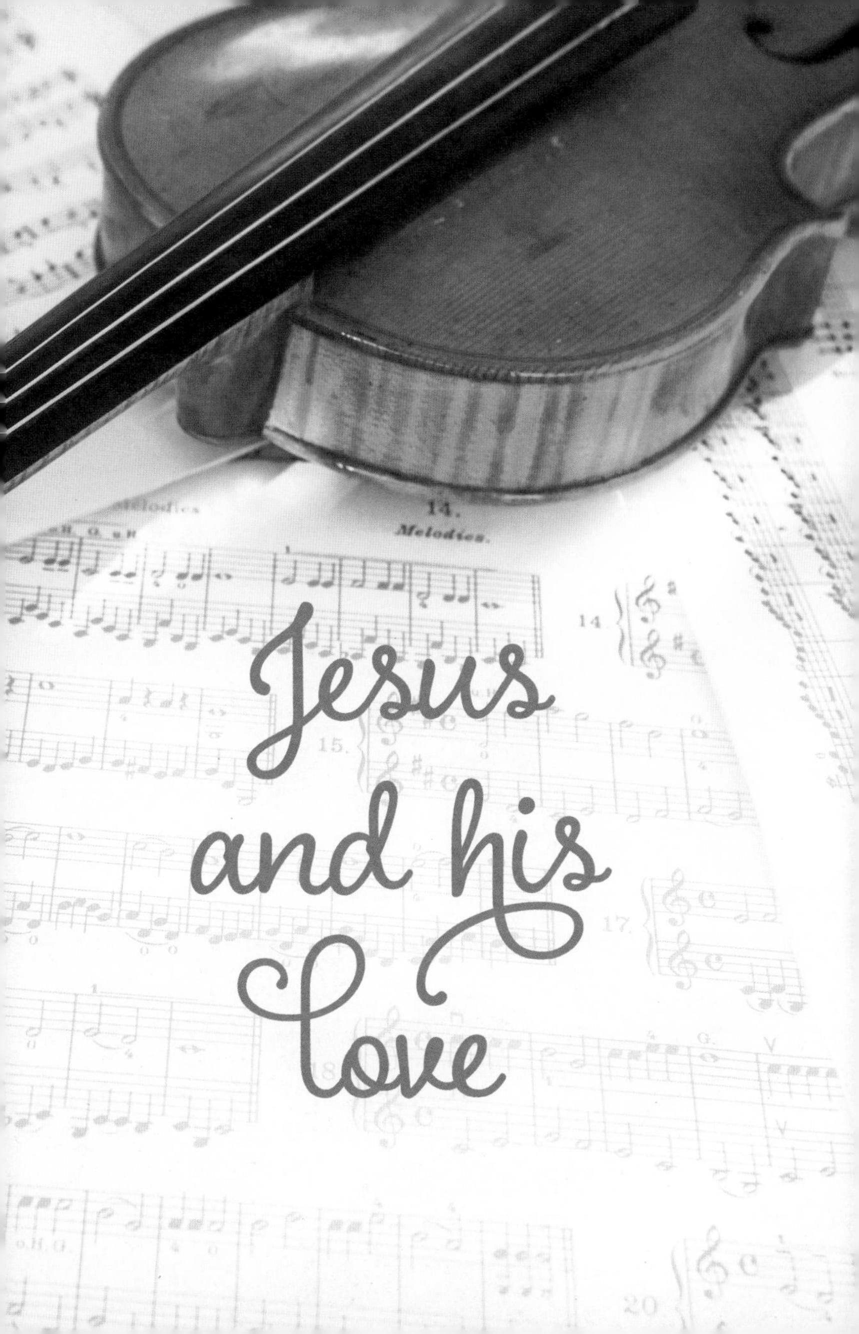

Count Your Blessings

Have you ever been caught by surprise in a sudden downpour? Even if you haven't experienced a physical drenching, you may be immersed in an emotional storm right now, with worrisome clouds swirling around you. Take heart in the assurance of this old gospel song: Whenever you think that "all is lost," the repeated chorus breaks through your despair with its exuberant joy: "Count your many blessings, name them one by one." Praise God! When you start thinking about God's gifts, the tally never seems to stop. Go ahead and remember all the ways God has blessed you.

Thank you, Lord, for being the sun shining through my storm. You generously provide for my needs. Let me realize how blessed I am each and every day.

GOD IS ABLE TO BLESS YOU ABUNDANTLY, SO THAT IN ALL THINGS
AT ALL TIMES, HAVING ALL THAT YOU NEED,
YOU WILL ABOUND IN EVERY GOOD WORK.

2 CORINTHIANS 9:8, NIV

It wasn't until he was in his late thirties that Johnson Oatman discovered an untapped musical talent: He was a natural-born songwriter. By the end of his life in 1922, he had left a blessing for generations to come: a legacy of more than five thousand gospel songs.

Pass Me Not

This beautiful, plaintive song by Fanny Crosby is based on the Bible story of two blind men who were sitting beside the road as Jesus left Jericho. When they called out to him for healing, the crowd tried to quiet them, but Jesus heard their cries and restored their sight. At times we all need healing. Maybe you're desperate right now, just as those blind men were. You know Jesus is out there, but you're unsure whether he hears you. Be assured that Jesus will always stop and listen. He will never pass you by, because he has promised, "I am with you always" (Matthew 28:20).

Jesus, whenever I'm at my wit's end and really don't know what to do, please send your help. I know you will answer my cry. You are my only hope.

"What do you want me to do for you?" [Jesus] asked.
"Lord," they answered, "we want our sight." Jesus had compassion
on them and touched their eyes. Immediately they received
their sight and followed him.

Matthew 20:32-34, niv

Fanny Crosby was trained to be independent, despite her blindness. She memorized Scripture easily, and when her ties with the New York Institution for the Blind opened the world of music to her, she learned to play several instruments. Add to this her knack for crafting inspirational lyrics, and the rest is gospel song history.

Save me by thy grace

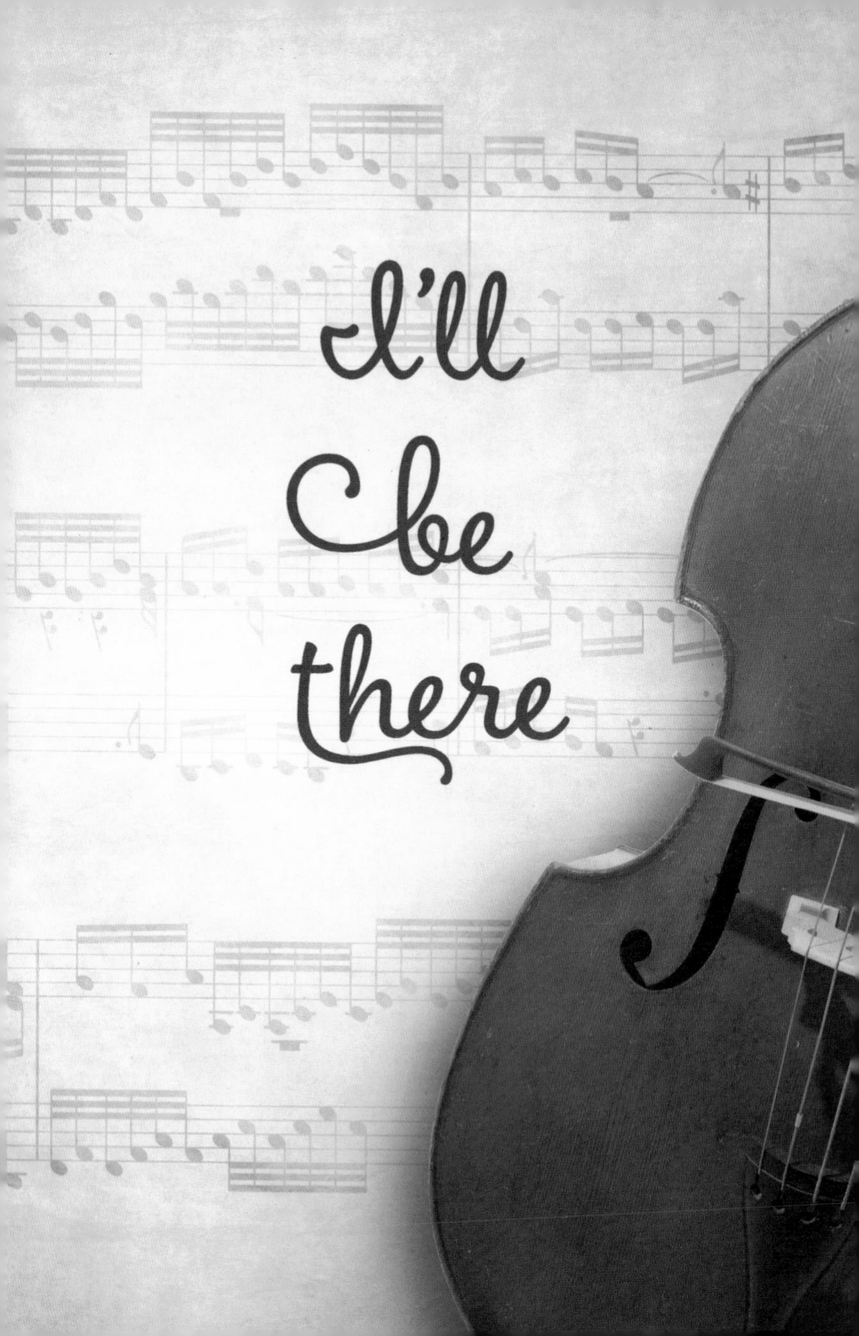
I'll be there

When the Roll Is Called Up Yonder

Of all the country versions of this gospel song, perhaps the one that best captures its exuberance is Loretta Lynn's rendition. Her vibrant voice, accompanied by musicians playing at a toe-tapping pace, captures the spirit of the song. You see, it's about God choosing you to be part of his family, one of his children. The "roll" is God's list of people who have turned from their sins and come to him. Have you become a follower of Jesus? Are you a child of God? If so, you will hear your name joyfully proclaimed.

Lord God, thank you for including me in your family.
Help me to know the rich meaning of being chosen by you and to live with joyful exuberance because I have the assurance of heaven.

THE LORD HIMSELF SHALL DESCEND FROM HEAVEN WITH A SHOUT, WITH THE VOICE OF THE ARCHANGEL, AND WITH THE TRUMP OF GOD.

1 THESSALONIANS 4:16, KJV

James Milton Black was a Sunday school teacher with a heart for children. When a young girl was absent one morning, Black visited her home and learned she was dying from pneumonia. Her serious illness was the inspiration for "When the Roll Is Called Up Yonder."

No One Ever Cared for Me Like Jesus

This song describes what we know to be true: Jesus' care is incomparable. There are down times, and then there are *really* down times. There are valleys, and then there are deep pits of despair. Perhaps you're in an emotional bottomless pit right now. Maybe you're grappling with some degree of depression. Christians are certainly not exempt from its devastating effects. Charles Weigle wrote this song based on his own real-life experience. His heartfelt words might be your thoughts too. Getting through your struggle is a complicated journey—a journey best walked with Jesus alongside you.

Lord Jesus, there are times when I hurt all over, and I know I can't make it without you. Thank you for holding me up so I can face another day.

GOD IS OUR MERCIFUL FATHER AND THE SOURCE OF ALL COMFORT. HE COMFORTS US IN ALL OUR TROUBLES SO THAT WE CAN COMFORT OTHERS.

2 CORINTHIANS 1:3-4

When Charles Weigle's wife tired of his evangelistic and songwriting ministry, she left him, taking their daughter. After five bleak years, Charles started writing songs again. One evening, sitting at his piano and reflecting on how God had cared for him during this difficult time, the music and lyrics for this song came to him.

A wondrous beauty I see

The Old Rugged Cross

Perhaps this familiar song is one you sang by heart as a child. Maybe it's time to sing it anew, to pay attention to its clear directive: "I'll cherish the old rugged cross, till my trophies at last I lay down." What are you holding on to in your life? What takes precedence over everything else? Nothing is more worth cherishing than Jesus' sacrifice on the cross, the event that changed history and still influences all that is to come. Now let's ask: Is anything else more important to you? Today, lay down all those other "trophies" and cling to the Cross of Jesus Christ.

Lord Jesus, thank you for dying for me on that rugged cross. Your death has given me new life. Help me to never forget the significance of what you did.

THE PREACHING OF THE CROSS IS TO THEM THAT PERISH FOOLISHNESS; BUT UNTO US WHICH ARE SAVED IT IS THE POWER OF GOD.

1 CORINTHIANS 1:18, KJV

Rev. George Bennard wrote this hymn, his most well-known, in 1913. It's also the focus of the The Old Rugged Cross Historical Museum in Reed City, Michigan, where the pastor and his wife retired. Several singers have inlcuded the hymn on their recordings, such as Ernest Tubb, Alan Jackson, and the Happy Goodmans.

Just As I Am

Most people consider "Just As I Am" as *the* "invitation" song—sung quietly at the end of a service as people come forward to receive Christ as their Savior. Actually, the hymn wasn't written with that intent in mind. One day in 1834, Charlotte Elliott was feeling useless because of a disability. Determined to remind herself of the truths of her faith, she wrote this hymn, bolstering her spirit with what the gospel message promises to all who accept it. Maybe you feel unworthy to be a child of God. Maybe you have questions and doubts. God beckons you to come just as you are.

Father God, I'm a mess. I don't feel worthy to even talk to you. Yet I know I need you more than I can express. I humbly ask you to accept me.

WHOEVER COMES TO ME I WILL NEVER CAST OUT.

JOHN 6:37, ESV

Charlotte Elliott was an English poet and hymn writer. Though "Just As I Am" became well known after publication in 1834, its popularity soared when Billy Graham made it the signature altar call song for his Crusades. At his conversion in 1934, Graham himself heard the hymn sung before he was convicted and walked down the aisle to accept Jesus.

He's a Personal Savior

When the group Southern Gospel A Cappella Project performs this song, you can't resist joining in the celebration of having a personal relationship with Jesus. What things in your life today can you celebrate because of Jesus? How has he blessed you? How has he touched your life, your heart? Make some time today to come to him. Instead of a shopping list, bring him a thank-you list—praises for what he's provided. Listen, talk, praise. And walk away cheerful and exuberant because you have a Savior who personally knows you and loves you.

Lord Jesus, thank you for _____. I praise you for _____. I am thrilled that I can come to you like this, that you love me and care for me.

O GIVE THANKS UNTO THE LORD; FOR HE IS GOOD:
FOR HIS MERCY ENDURETH FOR EVER.

PSALM 136:1, KJV

Lee Roy Abernathy was an innovative man. Besides writing this song, he is credited with creating a handbook for gospel musicians, printing the first gospel sheet music, and creating a popular mail-order piano course. He also was one of the first to employ "turnaround" introductions on songs.

Send the Light

"Send the Light" has inspired many Christians to become missionaries. The reference to the "Macedonian call" in the second stanza alludes to the apostle Paul's experience in Acts 16:9, where the Holy Spirit summons him there in a vision. You may not be called to a foreign country, but you *are* called to share the Good News where you are. Jesus said, "Ye are the light of the world." The prospect of sharing Jesus with others can be intimidating, but remember that God will give you the words. Ask him to direct you to friends and loved ones who are ready for the gospel message.

Lord God, I want to be an effective light for you. Give me courage, the right words, a compassionate heart, and the grace I need to tell others about Jesus.

YE ARE THE LIGHT OF THE WORLD. . . . LET YOUR LIGHT SO SHINE
BEFORE MEN, THAT THEY MAY SEE YOUR GOOD WORKS,
AND GLORIFY YOUR FATHER WHICH IS IN HEAVEN.
MATTHEW 5:14, 16, KJV

Charles Gabriel, a farmer's son, decided early on what his vocation would be; lyrics and melodies came easily to him. "Send the Light" was a commercial success, and he later wrote the tunes for "His Eye Is on the Sparrow" and "Will the Circle Be Unbroken?" Gabriel wrote or collaborated on at least seven thousand songs.

The
blessed
gospel
light

Hallowed be thy name

The Lord's Prayer

The 1935 melody of "The Lord's Prayer" has been performed in a variety of musical styles, from High Church choral to bluegrass. The Isaacs's a cappella performance at the Grand Ole Opry is both moving and mighty. Consider incorporating your favorite recording of this beloved song into your time with God. Play it once, letting the music and words wash over you. Then pray the words slowly, line by line, pausing and meditating on each phrase. Jesus connected with his Father directly and powerfully, and so can you.

Lord Jesus, thank you for teaching us how to pray. I'm learning that I don't need to use fancy words, because you desire honest conversation. Let me share what's on my heart.

OUR FATHER WHICH ART IN HEAVEN, HALLOWED BE THY NAME. THY KINGDOM COME. THY WILL BE DONE IN EARTH, AS IT IS IN HEAVEN. GIVE US THIS DAY OUR DAILY BREAD. AND FORGIVE US OUR DEBTS, AS WE FORGIVE OUR DEBTORS. AND LEAD US NOT INTO TEMPTATION, BUT DELIVER US FROM EVIL: FOR THINE IS THE KINGDOM, AND THE POWER, AND THE GLORY, FOR EVER. AMEN.

MATTHEW 6:9-13, KJV

Albert Hay Malotte was a musician and film composer who started his career as a theater organist for silent movies. Later he worked for Walt Disney Productions, where he wrote music for short animations. Malotte wrote several religious musical pieces, but his musical setting for "The Lord's Prayer" is his most memorable.

What a Day That Will Be

There's a saying that often appears on wall art, coffee mugs, and various other paraphernalia: "Dance like no one's watching. Love like you've never been hurt. Sing like no one's listening. Live like heaven is on earth." The promise of heaven is wonderful to dream about! But until that day comes, God wants you to reflect his glory and show others who Jesus is. Sing this song joyfully and hopefully. Someday you will see Jesus face-to-face. But for now, pray, "May your will be done on earth, as it is in heaven" (Matthew 6:10) and let his love shine through you.

Lord God, thank you for the promise of heaven. I can't wait to get there. But while I'm here on earth, help me boldly proclaim to others that you are "the way, the truth, and the life" (John 14:6).

HE WILL WIPE EVERY TEAR FROM THEIR EYES, AND THERE WILL BE
NO MORE DEATH OR SORROW OR CRYING OR PAIN.
ALL THESE THINGS ARE GONE FOREVER.
REVELATION 21:4

Jim Hill, the writer of "What a Day That Will Be," was a shoe salesman, a songwriter, and a singer with the Stamps, Statesmen, and Golden Keys quartets. When friends heard that Hill had died, they knew he was finally experiencing that glorious day he had been looking forward to.

I Need Thee Every Hour

Our need for God becomes desperate during a time of deep distress, whether it's a blast of bad news, the deepening fear of an unexpected diagnosis, or the sudden loss of a loved one. Perhaps you are enduring one of these situations or something similar right now. You're drowning emotionally and frantically as you pray for God's help. You don't know how you can even breathe without divine assistance. In these moments, hold on to him. Let him be your life preserver, supporting you hour by hour. Tell him what is hurting your heart right now, and release your burdens to him.

Father God, when devastation hits, it's hard to explain my despair.
I pray for the fortitude to get through difficult circumstances
that arise. Please reinforce me with your Spirit.

DO NOT BE AFRAID OR DISCOURAGED. FOR THE LORD YOUR GOD
IS WITH YOU WHEREVER YOU GO.

JOSHUA 1:9

Sensing God's nearness, Annie Hawks wrote the stanzas of this song and showed them to her pastor, Robert Lowry. Inspired, Lowry added a chorus and tune. Published in 1872, the hymn's appeal spread, and by the time of Hawks's death in 1918, it had been translated into more foreign languages than any other modern hymn.

Moment by Moment

It may have been a case of hymn writers' one-upmanship. The story goes that D. W. Whittle was talking with Henry Varley, a London preacher, at the 1893 World's Columbian Exposition in Chicago. Varley said he didn't like the hymn "I Need Thee Every Hour" very much because he needed the Lord *moment by moment*. That comment prompted Whittle to write this hymn. But you don't need to debate hours versus moments; the truth is that you need to walk with Jesus *all* the time. God promises to be with you, keeping you in his love every moment of every day.

Father God, too often I get so involved in my problems that I forget to ask you
for help. I am grateful you are available to me at any time.

CHRIST WILL MAKE HIS HOME IN YOUR HEARTS AS YOU TRUST
IN HIM. YOUR ROOTS WILL GROW DOWN INTO GOD'S LOVE
AND KEEP YOU STRONG.

EPHESIANS 3:17

D. W. Whittle was a Civil War veteran who was encouraged to become an evangelist by D. L. Moody. Whittle's daughter, May, who would eventually marry Moody's son Will, wrote the music for this song. Major Whittle wrote some two hundred hymns in his lifetime, including "Showers of Blessing."

Give the World a Smile

This bouncy, playful gospel tune celebrates the joy we have in Jesus, our Savior and friend. How often do you stop throughout the day to take a joy break with Jesus? As this song suggests, we should make time each day to share Jesus with others through a genuine smile. Our attitude toward people, our conversations with them, and our willingness to help are all reflections of the happiness that Jesus brings into our lives. Sure, we still have problems and frustrations . . . but Jesus is in our hearts, and that's the bottom line. Let his love be the reason you're smiling today.

Lord Jesus, thank you for all you are to me. Help me reflect to others the change you bring to my heart and the joy you bring to my life.

I HAVE TOLD YOU THESE THINGS SO THAT YOU WILL BE FILLED WITH MY JOY. YES, YOUR JOY WILL OVERFLOW!

JOHN 15:11

In the 1920s, Otis Deaton and M. L. Yandell were studying at the Stamps School of Music together. They collaborated on "Give the World a Smile," one of the first gospel songs to be played on the radio. In 1927, The Stamps Quartet recorded it, selling more than a million copies.

Love Lifted Me

This familiar gospel song, written in 1912, is inspired in part by the story of Jesus walking on water to join his disciples in their boat (Matthew 14:22-32). Peter jumps out and tries to walk toward Jesus on the stormy lake, but when his faith falters, he starts to sink. Immediately Jesus' loving hand catches Peter and saves him from drowning. We, too, are often caught in the storms of life, and our faith needs bolstering. Is a storm threatening to pull you under today? Let Jesus' love grasp you firmly. He'll lead you to safety and will never let you go.

God, I am dealing with so much right now, and I can't keep my head above water.
I rely on you to rescue me time and time again.

PETER WENT OVER THE SIDE OF THE BOAT AND WALKED ON THE WATER TOWARD JESUS. BUT WHEN HE SAW THE STRONG WIND AND THE WAVES, HE WAS TERRIFIED AND BEGAN TO SINK. "SAVE ME, LORD!" HE SHOUTED. JESUS IMMEDIATELY REACHED OUT AND GRABBED HIM.

MATTHEW 14:29-31

James Rowe was a lyricist and music journal editor in the early 1900s. He and Howard E. Smith wrote this song together in 1912. Rowe is said to have written more than nineteen thousand songs. In 1973, The Kingsmen Quartet released their album *Big and Live*, which included their compelling delivery of this song.

When
nothing else
could
help

Choose you this day

The Old White Flag

Be honest, now: Do you call the shots in your life, deciding what you'll do each day without giving a second thought to God? If so, how's that working for you? You might have accepted God's gift of salvation once, but lately you've been flying solo. Maybe it's time to examine your heart and repent, raising the flag of surrender to him. Doing so is not a sign of weakness, because the Lord exchanges your flag for a royal one. Be a proud flag bearer for him by letting him control your life.

Father God, when I live life on my terms, I make a mess of things. Help me to give you full rein in every aspect of my life. I humbly submit to you.

CHOOSE YOU THIS DAY WHOM YE WILL SERVE. . . . AS FOR ME AND MY HOUSE, WE WILL SERVE THE LORD.

JOSHUA 24:15, KJV

Plenty of white flags were waving when the Triumphant Quartet performed this Dianne Wilkinson song at the 2009 National Quartet Convention. The group received a Dove nomination that same year for Bluegrass Recorded Song of the Year. Wilkinson's decades-long contributions to gospel music began in the 1970s.

And Can It Be That I Should Gain?

Perhaps no hymn captures the sheer exhilaration of new life in Christ than this one. Though we don't use Charles Wesley's eighteenth-century language in our everyday speech, the song's intent is clear: What Christ did for us is incredible! Stop and think: God sent his Son to walk among us, to teach us, and to die in our place. Jesus saved us from the consequences of sin, redeeming us and restoring our relationship with the Father. Now we can spend eternity with him. I would consider that downright "amazing love," wouldn't you? Reignite the joy you experienced when you first said yes to Jesus.

Lord Jesus, I remember when I gave my life to you.
I couldn't stop talking about you. Restore and revive that initial excitement
in me, and help me to remain ever grateful.

———————

CHRIST SHALL BE MAGNIFIED IN MY BODY, WHETHER IT BE BY LIFE, OR BY DEATH. FOR TO ME TO LIVE IS CHRIST, AND TO DIE IS GAIN.

PHILIPPIANS 1:21, KJV

Charles Wesley was a prolific hymnist, to the tune of 8,989 songs. He was also a language scholar, a poet, a minister, and, alongside his brother John, a leader in the Methodist movement in eighteenth-century England. John Wesley described Charles's lyrics as having a "distinct and full account of scriptural Christianity." Praise be to God!

I'll Fly Away

This rousing tune is an all-time favorite sing-along at bluegrass festivals. The song is about realizing that the weariness of this life can be remedied only with the reality of eternal life with God. It reflects a deep, hopeful longing in the human heart. Perhaps you are exhausted by your life, too—tired from work and family responsibilities. While God doesn't promise an easy or untroubled earthly journey, he does promise that in his perfect timing he will open heaven and receive those who believe in him. Do you have a home waiting for you there?

Dear Jesus, some days I am completely done in. I don't know how I can work any longer or strive any harder. Please give me strength, energy, and determination to continue on.

THEN [JESUS] SAID, "I TELL YOU THE TRUTH, YOU WILL ALL SEE HEAVEN OPEN AND THE ANGELS OF GOD GOING UP AND DOWN ON THE SON OF MAN, THE ONE WHO IS THE STAIRWAY BETWEEN HEAVEN AND EARTH."

JOHN 1:51

In 1929, when Albert E. Brumley was working in an Oklahoma cotton field, he imagined escaping his backbreaking labor by flying away. "I'll Fly Away" has been recorded by countless musicians—from Southern Gospel groups to the Boston Pops Orchestra—and is just one of more than eight hundred of Brumley's inspirational songs.

In the Garden

One of the Bible's most poignant stories about Jesus' resurrection recounts Mary Magdalene grieving outside her Master's empty tomb. As she weeps, a man speaks to her. At first she mistakes him for the gardener and pleads for information about the location of Jesus' body. And then the stranger says her name (John 20:11, 14-16). Immediately Mary turns and recognizes her Lord. Maybe you, like Mary, are sorrowful right now, lamenting the loss of a job, a friend, a loved one. Jesus is standing right beside you, calling your name. Turn to him. He wants to tell you that you are "his own." Find your comfort in him.

Dear Jesus, I have lost so much in my life, and I am in deep pain. Thank you for being present and walking with me through this heartache.

HE ASKED HER, "WOMAN, WHY ARE YOU CRYING?
WHO IS IT YOU ARE LOOKING FOR?"

JOHN 20:15, NIV

The story goes that C. Austin Miles was sitting in a windowless basement one morning when he opened his Bible and the pages fell to John 20. Miles was so overcome with the powerful account of Mary Magdalene's personal encounter with Jesus that the lyrics and music for this song flowed effortlessly.

What a Friend We Have in Jesus

On a summer night at a small country church, participants in a hymn-sing are raising the roof with one gospel song request after another. Suddenly the pianist transitions into a lilting introduction, and the song leader says, "Let's sing, everyone, like we believe it." The congregation begins by expressing this simple assurance: "What a friend we have in Jesus." Maybe you're having a hard time right now because things just plain aren't right in your life. Even if you're feeling lonely, there is one person you can always count on. Whatever you are facing this moment, "take it to the Lord in prayer!"

Dear Jesus, _____ is weighing me down. I don't understand why these things are happening to me. Will you shoulder my burdens and hold me close? Thank you for always being there.

IF YOU ABIDE IN ME, AND MY WORDS ABIDE IN YOU,
ASK WHATEVER YOU WISH, AND IT WILL BE DONE FOR YOU.
JOHN 15:7, ESV

Born in Ireland in 1819, Joseph Scriven would experience several tragic losses during his lifetime. His first fiancée drowned, and later his second fiancée died suddenly. When his mother became ill, Scriven wrote a poem, "Pray without Ceasing," to console her. Its lyrics are the basis for the hymn we're familiar with today.

Soon and Very Soon

The Imperials' version of this Andraé Crouch song starts with a jazzy intro, then launches into the tight harmonies the quartet is known for. The song anticipates the day when we'll see our King in heaven. Another truth Crouch adds is that God knows his people by name. Jesus, our Shepherd, expounds on this in John 10:3: "The sheep recognize his voice and come to him. He calls his own sheep by name." God not only knows your name but is also tenderly calling you. When was the last time you called out *his* name?

Almighty King, I am thankful to be your child and rejoice that I will join you in eternity. You know me intimately. Keep reminding me of your love.

I KNEW YOU BEFORE I FORMED YOU IN YOUR MOTHER'S WOMB.
BEFORE YOU WERE BORN I SET YOU APART.
JEREMIAH 1:5

At fifteen, Andraé Crouch wrote his first song, "The Blood Will Never Lose Its Power." In 1971, Andraé's group, Andraé Crouch and The Disciples, released their first album, *Take the Message Everywhere*. Crouch took the gospel message seriously and he changed the landscape of contemporary Christian music.

I set you apart

Raised To new Life

Turn Your Eyes upon Jesus

The chorus of this slow, reflective song is beautifully poetic, taking its inspiration from a booklet titled *Focussed*, by artist, writer, and missionary to Algeria, Lilias Trotter. At the end of the meditation, Trotter encourages readers to "Turn full your soul's vision to Jesus, and look and look at Him, and a strange dimness will come over all that is apart from Him." When Helen Lemmel read those words, the song practically wrote itself. Maybe it's a good time to reassess your priorities and follow what truly matters. Take time right now to sit at Jesus' feet, and see what he wants you to learn.

Lord Jesus, I want to focus on you because you are Almighty God—
the most important person in my life. Help me to pay attention
to everything you say and direct me to do.

Since you have been raised to new life with Christ, set sights on the realities of heaven, where Christ sits in the place of honor at God's right hand. Think about the things of heaven, not the things of earth.

COLOSSIANS 3:1-2

Helen Lemmel, born in England in 1864, moved to the United States with her family when she was twelve. Lemmel became an accomplished singer, a musician, and a hymn writer, performing at churches across the country. Lemmel eventually taught voice at Moody Bible Institute and the Bible Institute of Los Angeles.

Leaning on the Everlasting Arms

Imagine a shepherd looking for a lost lamb. He trudges across fields, searching for the stray. Finally he finds the cold and trembling animal. The shepherd reaches down, gathers it up, and cradles it in his arms. They are strong arms, yet his touch is tender. They are arms that offer shelter. Jesus is the "great Shepherd of the sheep" who "ratified an eternal covenant with his blood" (Hebrews 13:20). That covenant of salvation was with us, his sheep. Some days, quite frankly, we are as scared as lost lambs. We need Jesus to hold us tightly. Is that what you need today?

Dear Jesus, I am scared and need you near me right now. The comfort of your arms makes me feel safe and secure. Thank you for your protective love.

HE TENDS HIS FLOCK LIKE A SHEPHERD: HE GATHERS THE LAMBS IN HIS ARMS
AND CARRIES THEM CLOSE TO HIS HEART.

ISAIAH 40:11, NIV

This hymn was a collaborative effort. Music teacher A. J. Showalter was searching for inspiration to comfort two students whose wives had died when he was moved by the image of God's "everlasting arms" in Deuteronomy 33:27. Showalter's lines are the hymn's refrain. The stanzas were written by pastor and hymn writer E. A. Hoffman.

Times of
refreshing
shall
come

Please Forgive Me

Are you having restless nights instead of restful ones? Maybe there are things you've done that haunt you, that mire you in regret, second-guessing, and guilt. You can't stop playing them over and over in your head. In the agony of these experiences, you cry out to God for forgiveness, perhaps in desperation or as a whispered last hope. The Bible says God is "merciful and forgiving" (Daniel 9:9), so take heart in this promise. Know that in this moment, when you confess your sins, God will forgive you and receive you into his arms.

God, I hesitate to come to you because I am filthy with sin. Yet I need your cleansing forgiveness. Thank you for never turning your back on me.

REPENT YE THEREFORE, AND BE CONVERTED, THAT YOUR SINS MAY
BE BLOTTED OUT, WHEN THE TIMES OF REFRESHING SHALL COME
FROM THE PRESENCE OF THE LORD.

ACTS 3:19, KJV

The words of this song are personal for Gerald Crabb. As a pastor and evangelist, he had gone through a divorce and was struggling with alcoholism. The guilt of his sins overwhelmed him one day while he was working at his car wash, and he fell to his knees in tears. God met him there. His testimony of God's grace was wrapped in this number one hit for Singing News Radio. Crabb has reached this milestone more times than any other Southern Gospel songwriter.

Because He Lives

The work of Jesus on the cross is more than just a ticket to heaven. Jesus changes everything for us in our daily struggles and worries . . . because he lives. Our risen Lord provides just what we need each and every day. He has overcome the world. What do Jesus' death and resurrection mean to you? Have the truths they embody changed your life? Jesus does make life worth living. Reflect on how he has done that for you.

Lord Jesus, you have given me joy, pleasure, and deep satisfaction—because you live in me. I humbly thank you for your atoning death and resurrection.

YET A LITTLE WHILE AND THE WORLD WILL SEE ME NO MORE, BUT YOU WILL SEE ME. BECAUSE I LIVE, YOU ALSO WILL LIVE.

JOHN 14:19, ESV

Bill and Gloria Gaither were expecting their third baby in 1970, when the nation was in chaos from the Vietnam War, decaying morals, and questions about God's existence. Who would want to bring a child into a world teetering on instability? As the couple continued to struggle with doubts, they were intrigued by a single blade of grass that had pushed through their office's recently blacktopped parking lot. It assured them of the firm hope of the Resurrection, and "Because He Lives" was their personal response.

The work of your fingers

How Big Is God

Hopefully the problems you face are, as they say in the South, "no higher than corn and no lower than taters." Yet sometimes the challenges of life seem immense, as unending as the universe itself. Listen to John Hall's performance of "How Big Is God." His booming bass voice represents well the deep and vast God he is singing about. God is the ruler of heaven and earth, yet personal enough to live inside you. This story of the almighty God loving each one of us is woven throughout the entire Bible. Now, how big is your love for him?

Lord of all and Lord of my life, I can't begin to grasp
how infinite you are, and yet you are my personal Shepherd
who guides me. I am humbled by your love for me.

WHEN I LOOK AT YOUR HEAVENS, THE WORK OF YOUR FINGERS, THE MOON
AND THE STARS, WHICH YOU HAVE SET IN PLACE, WHAT IS MAN THAT YOU
ARE MINDFUL OF HIM, AND THE SON OF MAN THAT YOU CARE FOR HIM?
YET YOU HAVE MADE HIM A LITTLE LOWER THAN THE HEAVENLY BEINGS AND
CROWNED HIM WITH GLORY AND HONOR.

PSALM 8:3-5, ESV

Stuart Hamblen had a varied career as a popular songwriter, radio personality, Hollywood actor, and country and western singer. At midlife, he attended a Billy Graham crusade that eventually led him to turn his life over to the Lord. Hamblen's song "It Is No Secret" topped the gospel, country, and pop charts in 1950.

Hide Thou Me

Have you ever thought, *If only I could get away from my life . . .* ? You might take a personal day off work, but that's not always enough, is it? When you're discouraged, you want to hide from it all. The psalmist David had plenty of those moments in his life, but he trusted in God, declaring, "He will hide me in his sanctuary." David's experience is relevant for us today. In him, you can find your escape, your protection, your respite. Rather than planning an extravagant vacation, maybe consider taking some days off to shelter in the place of the Rock: Jesus himself.

> *Lord Jesus, it is so easy to feel crushed by concerns at times.*
> *When I feel the desire to get away from it all, help me find*
> *a way to retreat from the world with you.*

IN YOU, LORD, I HAVE TAKEN REFUGE; LET ME NEVER BE PUT TO SHAME;
DELIVER ME IN YOUR RIGHTEOUSNESS. TURN YOUR EAR TO ME, COME
QUICKLY TO MY RESCUE; BE MY ROCK OF REFUGE, A STRONG FORTRESS TO
SAVE ME. SINCE YOU ARE MY ROCK AND MY FORTRESS, FOR THE SAKE OF
YOUR NAME LEAD AND GUIDE ME.

PSALM 31:1-3, NIV

"Hide Thou Me" was written in 1926 by L. R. Tolbert and Thoro Harris. Harris was one of the most creative African American hymn writers of the early 1900s. The slower tempo is a change of pace from most Southern Gospel songs, which makes it a favorite.

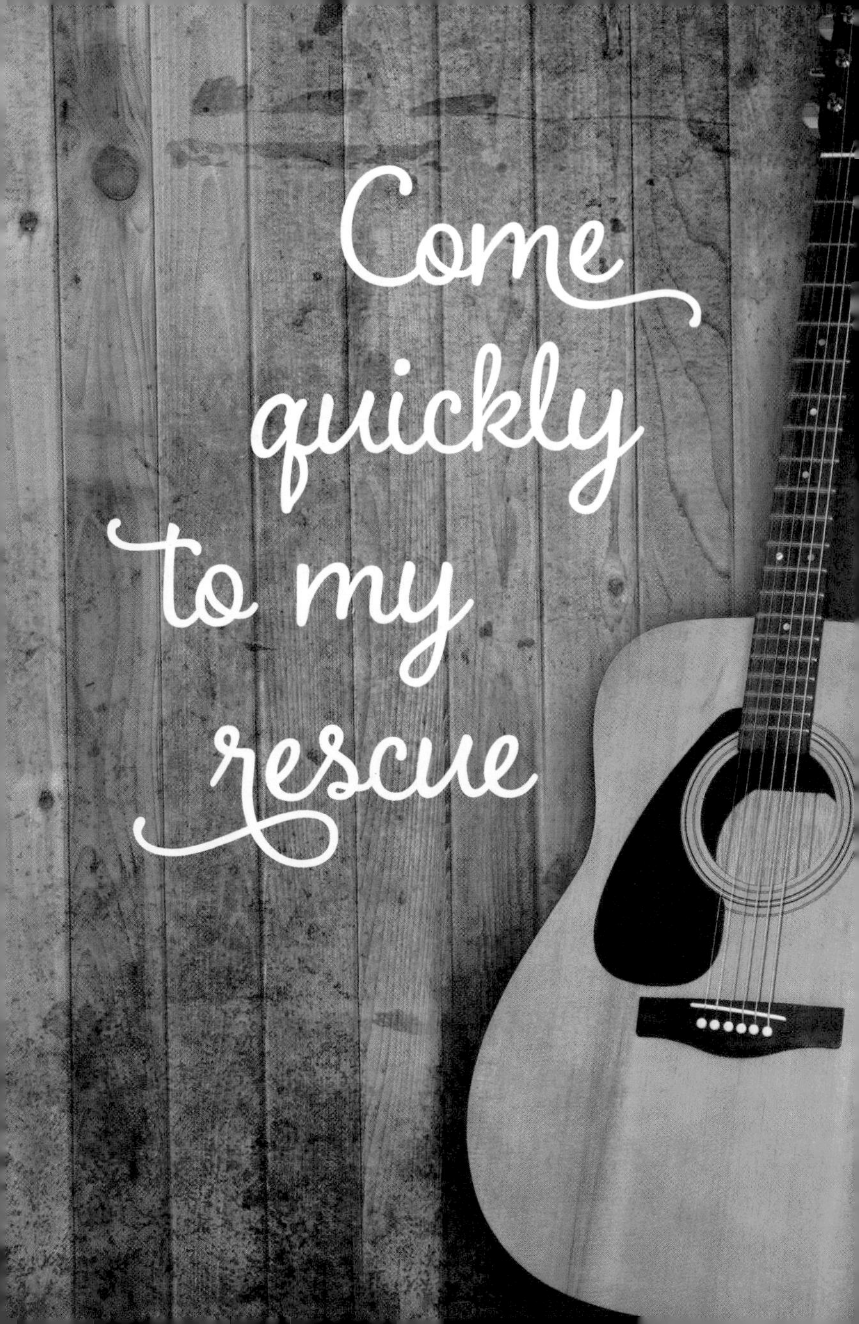
Come quickly to my rescue

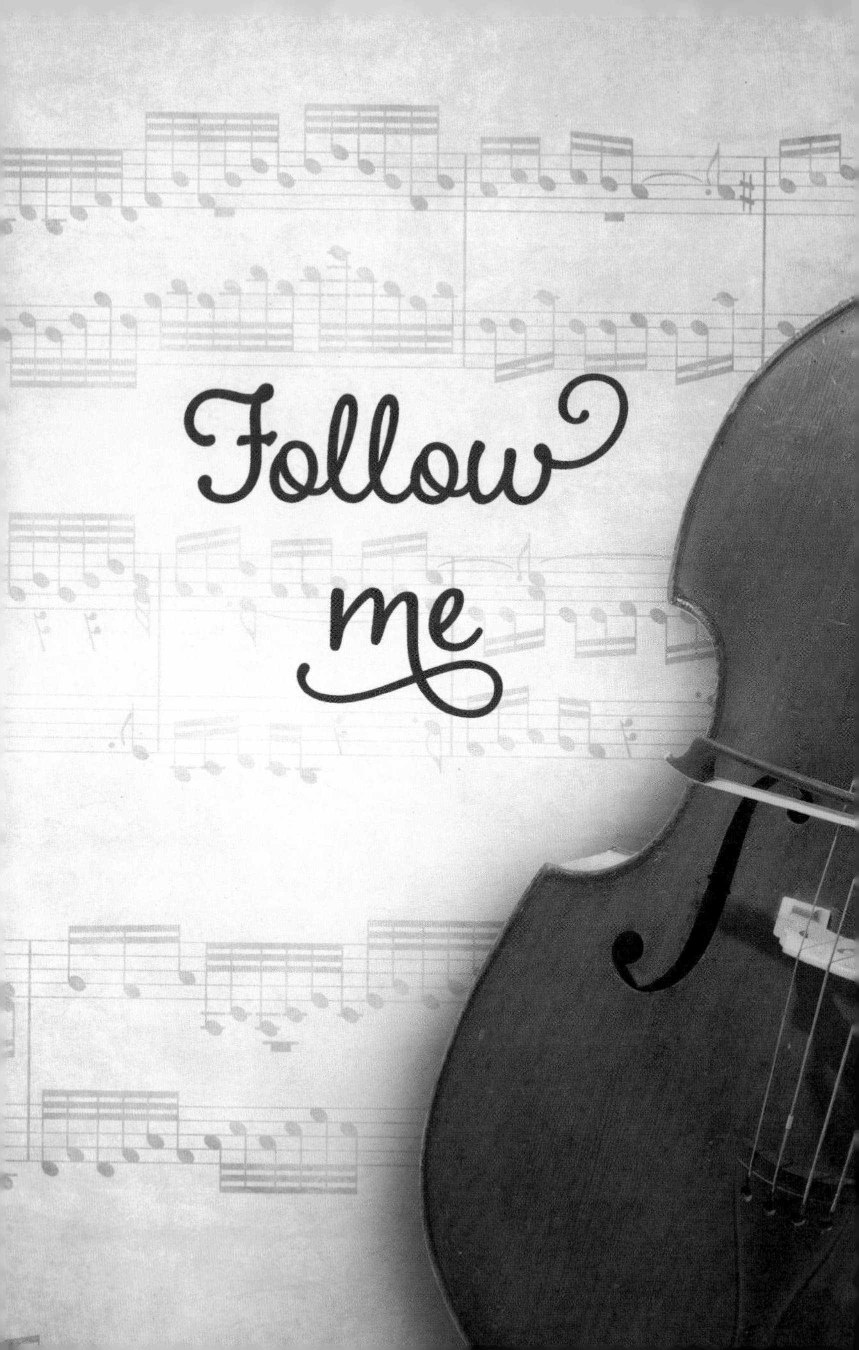
Follow
me

I'd Rather Have Jesus

What does following Jesus mean to you? Some may claim to be Christians, yet give just a passing nod to Jesus. Others start out with fervent passion for Jesus but later cool and wander off, lured by riches or fame. A precious few understand the high price of true discipleship. For many followers, even today, that kind of allegiance has cost them their lives. Which description fits you? Are you willing to truly let God lead you? George Beverly Shea, who composed the music to this song, was compelled to do so. Maybe now is the time for you to reignite your commitment to Jesus.

Jesus, I'm guilty of trying to find fulfillment in earthly possessions that don't satisfy. I want to renew my decision to follow you. Help me to let go of selfish interests and hold on to you.

IF ANY MAN WILL COME AFTER ME, LET HIM DENY HIMSELF, AND TAKE UP HIS CROSS, AND FOLLOW ME. FOR WHOSOEVER WILL SAVE HIS LIFE SHALL LOSE IT: AND WHOSOEVER WILL LOSE HIS LIFE FOR MY SAKE SHALL FIND IT.

MATTHEW 16:24-25, KJV

Famed singer and composer George Beverly Shea was twenty-three when he found a copy of Rhea Miller's poem, handwritten by his mother, on the family piano. Immediately Shea matched its words to a melody he felt in his heart. His mother had been praying that George would decline a secular singing job he was considering. He did, launching a celebrated gospel music career.

The Healer Hasn't Lost His Touch

This gospel song, popularized by the Tribute Quartet, speaks of doubters who are questioning and broken people who are waiting for healing. These are not exclusively nonbelievers; sometimes Christians find themselves wondering whether God cares. Has your faith fractured because of physical suffering? Turn to the Gospels and read about how Jesus healed people. He astonished the doubters—even his own disciples—with the power of his touch. These were not just bodies that were healed but also hearts and souls. Whatever you're experiencing right now, Jesus can heal you. He certainly hasn't lost his power. Let him attend to your need.

Jesus, I humbly ask for a miraculous healing of my body, soul, and spirit. Stay close beside me. That is the only way I can become whole.

FOR YOU WHO FEAR MY NAME, THE SUN OF RIGHTEOUSNESS
WILL RISE WITH HEALING IN HIS WINGS.

MALACHI 4:2

This song by Jason Cox, Joseph Habedank, and Tony Wood was a perfect choice for the Tribute Quartet, released to radio as a single that shot to number one on the Southern Gospel radio charts. In 2020, the group received an unprecedented nine nominations in different categories for the Singing News Fan Awards.

Great Is Thy Faithfulness

Sometimes it seems that our friends aren't really friends and the ones we love don't love us back. In times like these, the last place we'd think to go for a word of comfort is the book of Lamentations. Its chapters contain one lament after another. Yet in the middle of chapter 3, we see the realization of God's love breaking through: "His compassions never fail. They are new every morning; great is your faithfulness" (Lamentations 3:22-23, NIV). These words are the source of a hymn that has been sung—often tearfully—by millions, bringing them solace and comfort. God's faithfulness never wavers.

God, my heart is aching from disappointment and loss. But I thank you, Lord, for being there for me even when my faith is weak.

EVERY GOOD GIFT AND EVERY PERFECT GIFT IS FROM ABOVE, AND COMETH DOWN FROM THE FATHER OF LIGHTS, WITH WHOM IS NO VARIABLENESS, NEITHER SHADOW OF TURNING.

JAMES 1:17, KJV

Songwriter Thomas Chisholm struggled his entire life with a meager income and poor health. Still, he found hope in God and his Word and expressed it in poems. In 1923, he sent a collection of his works to musician William Runyan, who put "Great Is Thy Faithfulness" to music. The hymn was later popularized by Billy Graham.

When I Survey the Wondrous Cross

This hymn, written in the 1700s by an English Congregational minister and theologian, seems an unlikely candidate for Southern Gospel, yet its marvelous harmonies make it a quartet favorite. But there's something more that sets it apart. The writer begins with a prayerful self-reflection focused on the meaning of the Cross, and it leads him to a profound understanding of its significance: Jesus' sacrifice "demands my soul, my life, my all." Yes, the Cross is extremely personal. Jesus died for the sins of the world, including yours. Ponder his wondrous act of love and what it means for you.

Jesus, I can't begin to fathom what you willingly did for me by taking my sin upon yourself. You redeemed me from eternal separation from God. I'm humbly grateful to be embraced by your love.

HE CANCELED THE RECORD OF THE CHARGES AGAINST US AND TOOK IT AWAY BY NAILING IT TO THE CROSS.

COLOSSIANS 2:14

From a young age, Isaac Watts was adept at creating rhymes. Later, as a hymnist, he used that gift to transform eighteenth-century church music, which was mostly based on the Psalms, with fresh language for congregational worship. This hymn, considered by many as his finest, draws from Psalm 90.

Turn Your Radio On

When you hear the Statler Brothers perform this song—a catchy tune with full harmonies and playful pauses—you know it was created for Southern Gospel. And it's evident the group is enjoying singing this classic. Each time they approach the end of the chorus, there is a momentary silence before Harold Reid's sonorous bass reminds us we need to have clear communication with God, tuning out everything but him. This should be a daily thing, don't you think? What about right now? Are you listening to God? Find a quiet place, and prayerfully open your heart to what he wants to say to you.

Dear Lord, what do you want me to hear from you today?
I am listening in earnest for your voice, your words,
and your direction. Please make your way clear to me.

IN ALL THY WAYS ACKNOWLEDGE HIM,
AND HE SHALL DIRECT THY PATHS.
PROVERBS 3:6, KJV

Albert Brumley's first paid job with the Hartford Music Company earned him $12.50 a month as a staff writer. Later the Stamps-Baxter Music Company offered him a contract to write a dozen songs per year for $20.00 a month. "Turn Your Radio On" was one he wrote for them in 1938.

I Surrender All

"All I need today is a little bit of sweet tea and a whole lot of Jesus" is a common Southern saying. Sounds good, and yet for many of us that "little bit" of whatever is actually a pretty big thing we hold on to as more important than him. So here are two questions: What is your most important pursuit in life, and are you willing to give it up if it's not God's will? God isn't a killjoy; he doesn't want to deprive you of what you enjoy. But real happiness comes only in total obedience and surrender to him. That's what will bring you ultimate fulfillment.

Lord Jesus, help me to think of the things I can't let go of in my life.
Please convict me and give me courage to relinquish anything that displeases you.

I BESEECH YOU THEREFORE, BRETHREN, BY THE MERCIES OF GOD, THAT YE
PRESENT YOUR BODIES A LIVING SACRIFICE, HOLY, ACCEPTABLE UNTO GOD,
WHICH IS YOUR REASONABLE SERVICE.

ROMANS 12:1, KJV

Judson van DeVenter was a passionate artist and art teacher as well as a musician and composer. When Van DeVenter felt called to become an evangelist, he struggled to give up his art career. Five years later, he said yes to God and devoted himself to full-time Christian service.

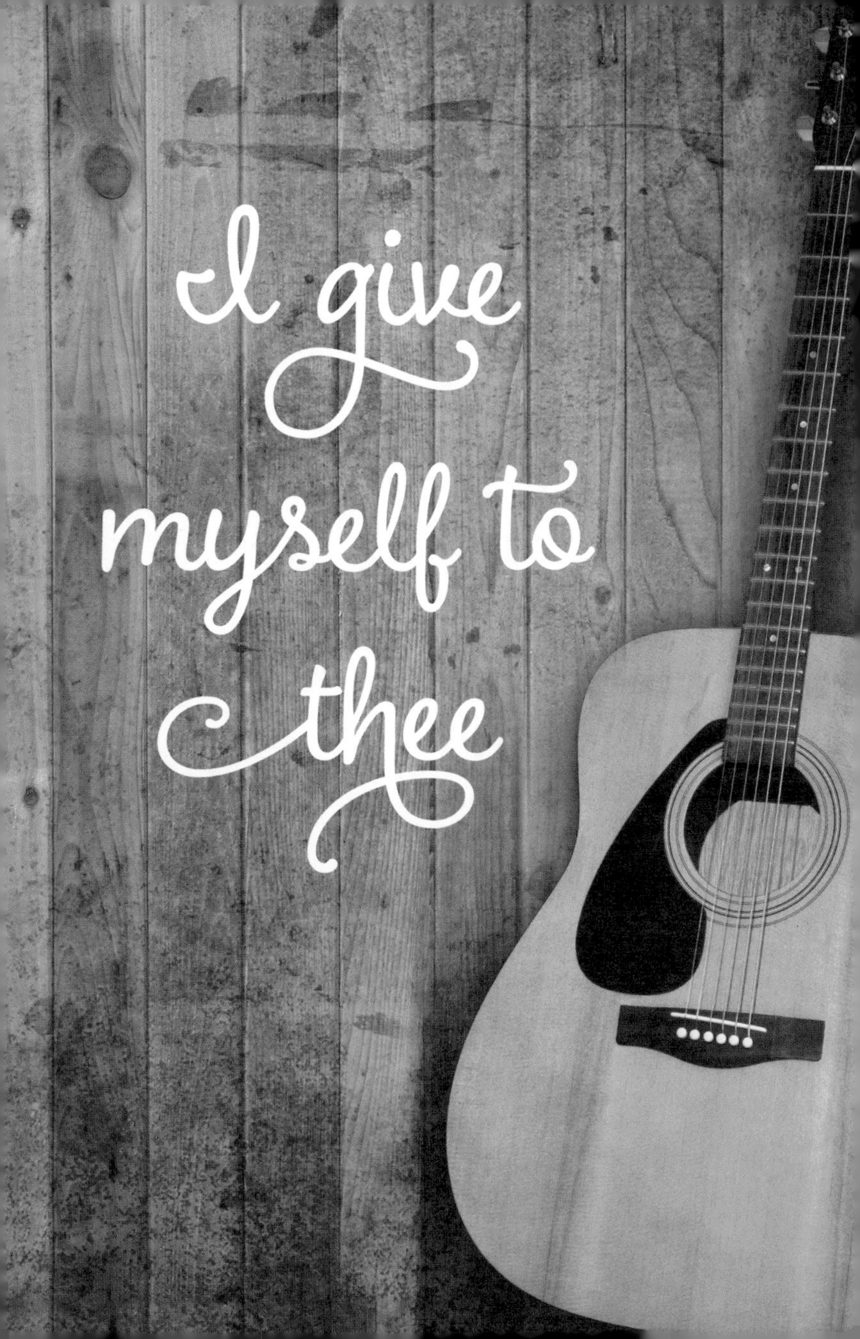
I give
myself to
thee

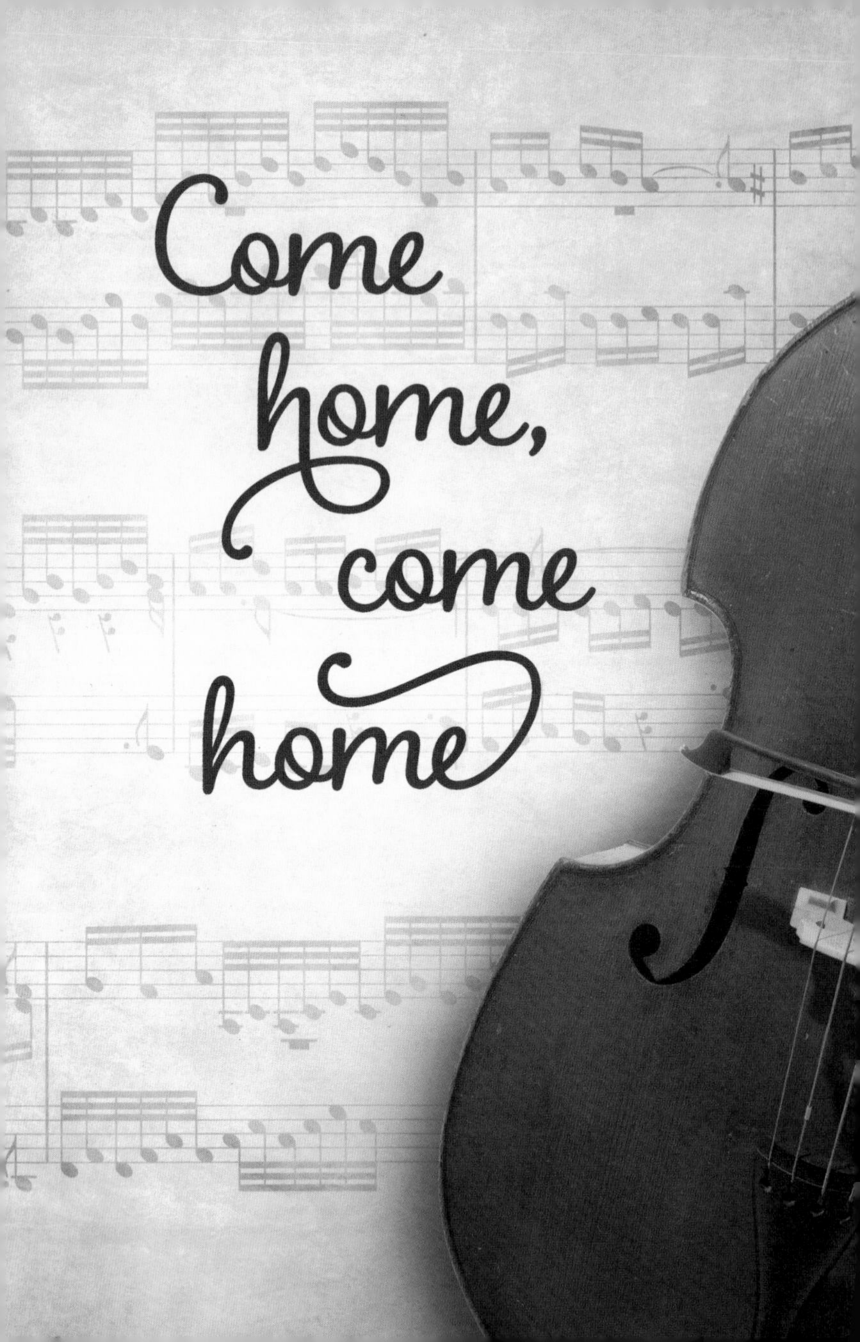
Come home, come home

Softly and Tenderly

This beloved song, written more than a century ago, has been used as an invitation hymn, similar to "Just As I Am." It compels sinners to come to Jesus, God's Son, who died on the cross to make atonement for the sins of the entire world. But its words also comfort people in their daily lives. The moment your heart cries out to God and you come into his presence, he tenderly greets you. He's been calling you, watching for you, anticipating your arrival as you come home. Has it been a while since you've spent time together? His pardon and love await you.

Lord Jesus, during times of uncertainty, I'm thankful you are always accessible. You give me courage and resolve to go on. Please continue to guide me.

WHEN DOUBTS FILLED MY MIND, YOUR COMFORT
GAVE ME RENEWED HOPE AND CHEER.

PSALM 94:19

Will L. Thompson grew up in East Liverpool, Ohio. In his early years, the versatile songwriter wrote patriotic songs and music for minstrel performers. This hymn—his most famous—was published in 1880 through his own music publishing company. Thompson's other notable hymn is "Jesus Is All the World to Me."

The Love of God

Do you ever wonder how God could love you? Perhaps you are painfully aware of how much you've strayed and have convinced yourself that you're disqualified from having a relationship with him. But the Bible says, "Neither death nor life, nor angels nor rulers, nor things present nor things to come, nor powers, nor height nor depth, nor anything else in all creation, will be able to separate us from the love of God in Christ Jesus our Lord" (Romans 8:38-39, ESV). Know this: God wants you. When you turn away from sin and run into his arms, he forgives you. He loves you—without limits.

Father God, I am ashamed of the things I've done that have grieved your heart.
Please forgive me and flood my heart with your unconditional love.

SEE WHAT KIND OF LOVE THE FATHER HAS GIVEN TO US,
THAT WE SHOULD BE CALLED CHILDREN OF GOD; AND SO WE ARE.
1 JOHN 3:1, ESV

Around 1917, Frederick M. Lehman, a Nazarene pastor, heard an evangelist end his message with a poem found written by a patient on an insane asylum wall. Later it was discovered that the words were adapted from an Aramaic poem by an eleventh-century rabbi. The words became the starting point for this hymn.

How measureless and strong!

God
in three
persons

Holy, Holy, Holy

If you've only sung this as a congregational hymn, you might want to sample The Martins' energetic a cappella version. It's an all-out celebration of the Father, Son, and Holy Spirit. But what does the Holy Trinity mean to us on a practical level? Here's one way to look at it: The Father who created us fully engaged himself to bridge the gulf between us and intimately connect with us. He sent his Son, Jesus, to rescue us from sin, and he provides his Spirit to guide and comfort. There's much about the Trinity we don't understand, but that shouldn't stop us from proclaiming, "Blessed Trinity!"

Lord God, I come to you humbly, with thanksgiving and praise. Thank you for creating me, redeeming me, and reminding me of your love through the Holy Spirit. I'm in awe of your mercy.

THIS IS HE WHO CAME BY WATER AND BLOOD—JESUS CHRIST; NOT ONLY BY WATER, BUT BY WATER AND BLOOD. AND IT IS THE SPIRIT WHO BEARS WITNESS, BECAUSE THE SPIRIT IS TRUTH. FOR THERE ARE THREE THAT BEAR WITNESS IN HEAVEN: THE FATHER, THE WORD, AND THE HOLY SPIRIT; AND THESE THREE ARE ONE.

1 JOHN 5:6-7, NKJV

Oxford-educated, Reginald Heber was an accomplished poet in the early 1800s, inspired by William Cowper's hymns to write his own. Heber didn't write a vast number of hymns, but "Holy, Holy, Holy" remains one of the most revered worship songs to this day. Heber was appointed Bishop of Calcutta, dying in India three years later.

He Hideth My Soul

This endearing hymn by Fanny Crosby is a Southern Gospel standard. Its lyrics are inspired by the time when Moses said to the Lord, "Show me your glorious presence" (Exodus 33:18). Since no human could glimpse God's face without dying, the Lord hid Moses in a rock crevice and shielded him with his hand as he passed by. From infancy, Fanny Crosby's eyes were covered by blindness, yet she was able to "see" God's glory and infuse it into her songs. God's intimate care will allow you to see his glory—as much as you need but not more than you can bear.

Lord God, thank you for your loving presence. Help me to understand the parts of you I cannot see and to trust in your protecting and saving grace.

I WILL CAUSE ALL MY GOODNESS TO PASS IN FRONT OF YOU, AND . . . I WILL HAVE MERCY ON WHOM I WILL HAVE MERCY, AND I WILL HAVE COMPASSION ON WHOM I WILL HAVE COMPASSION. . . . WHEN MY GLORY PASSES BY, I WILL PUT YOU IN A CLEFT IN THE ROCK AND COVER YOU WITH MY HAND UNTIL I HAVE PASSED BY.

EXODUS 33:19, 22, NIV

Fanny Crosby was a poet who taught English grammar, rhetoric, and history at the New York Institution for the Blind. Musical talent abounded in her family. Members oversaw singing schools and published songs, and one future crooner even became a star. It's not surprising that Fanny would also be a natural at songwriting.

We Shall See Jesus

Listening to The Cathedrals perform their dramatic interpretation of this song, you can't help but wonder, *What if I had been there when Jesus performed miracles? What if I had watched Jesus walk to the cross? What if I had witnessed his resurrection and ascension firsthand?* If you had seen Jesus in person, would it have changed your relationship with him? And yet you have seen him in your life, felt his hand upon you. Jesus is as real and alive today as he was two thousand years ago. Hold on to that truth, and wait expectantly for his triumphant return.

Lord Jesus, help me to remember those times you have helped me—more times than I can count. I thank you now, and I'll thank you in person one day.

BELOVED, WE ARE GOD'S CHILDREN NOW, AND WHAT WE WILL BE HAS NOT YET APPEARED; BUT WE KNOW THAT WHEN HE APPEARS WE SHALL BE LIKE HIM, BECAUSE WE SHALL SEE HIM AS HE IS.

1 JOHN 3:2, ESV

Dianne Wilkinson believes gospel songs should be evangelistic and comforting and that they should glorify God. The Southern Gospel Music Association awarded "We Shall See Jesus" Song of the Year honors in 1984. In 2000, Wilkinson became the first woman nominated as Songwriter of the Year by the Association.

Victory in Jesus

What do you need victory over today? What battle are you fighting? Maybe it's been a lifelong struggle, and your goal is to get through one more day. Perhaps it's a temptation that's confronting you this very moment. This song speaks of the victory over sin that Jesus won for you on the cross. Through faith in his sacrifice, he gives you the power and grace to overcome what you're up against. The Bible says, "Every child of God defeats this evil world, and we achieve this victory through our faith" (1 John 5:4). Put on God's armor (Ephesians 6:10-18), and follow your triumphant leader, Jesus.

God, you know every challenge I am dealing with. I know your strength will help me keep fighting. I pray in the name of Jesus for victory over the enemy.

DON'T BE AFRAID, FOR I AM WITH YOU. DON'T BE DISCOURAGED, FOR I AM YOUR GOD. I WILL STRENGTHEN YOU AND HELP YOU. I WILL HOLD YOU UP WITH MY VICTORIOUS RIGHT HAND.

ISAIAH 41:10

E. M. Bartlett's contribution to Southern Gospel music is significant. He cofounded the Hartford Music Company in 1918 and opened the Hartford Music Institute in 1921, personally mentoring Albert Brumley. Bartlett stopped touring after he suffered a stroke in 1939 that left him bedridden, but his deep faith inspired this final song.

I will hold you up

All
the stars
obey

I Sing the Mighty Power of God

The Ball Brothers' rendition of this beloved church hymn is thrilling—there's no doubt the vocalists are giving glory and honor to God. During times when we feel weak and powerless, it's worth listening to their performance again and returning to the Bible to be reminded of who God really is. Jesus once accused religious leaders of underestimating the power of God because they did not know the Scriptures (Matthew 22:29). Maybe we do that too. When we're not spending time with God by reading his Word daily, we can forget all he has done. Take time to plug into his power each and every day.

God, help me to recognize your authority and to live confidently because I am your child. I have seen how your power that makes mountains rise can also change a person's life.

THE KINGDOM OF GOD IS NOT JUST A LOT OF TALK;
IT IS LIVING BY GOD'S POWER.

I CORINTHIANS 4:20

> Isaac Watts is often called the father of English hymnody. Watts loved children, and he wrote this hymn for them to sing, giving them a visual idea of God as the great Creator. Watts probably didn't expect that it would become even more popular with adults as a worship song.

Just a Little Talk with Jesus

The Oak Ridge Boys' rendition of this song is spirited and fun. But the song's advice is worth taking seriously. Life can be tense at times—not always because of one big thing but because of an accumulation of little frustrations and problems. Are you experiencing that right now? If so, then now is a perfect time to have a one-on-one with the Lord. Don't hold back; express all your concerns to him. Think about starting every day this way. All your worries won't magically disappear, but Jesus will help you put everything in perspective, easing your mind.

Jesus, I come to you with many anxieties and fears—
too many to count. May I tell you what is keeping me up at night?
I need your comfort and guidance right now.

HUMBLE YOURSELVES THEREFORE UNDER THE MIGHTY HAND OF GOD, THAT HE MAY EXALT YOU IN DUE TIME: CASTING ALL YOUR CARE UPON HIM; FOR HE CARETH FOR YOU.

1 PETER 5:6-7, KJV

Cleavant Derricks wrote this popular tune in 1937 and sold it to Stamps-Baxter Music Company in exchange for fifty songbooks that he sold for a dime apiece. Derricks didn't record the song himself until 1975, but countless others did. The Oak Ridge Boys won a Grammy in 1978 for their recording.

Magnify
the
Lord

It Is Well with My Soul

Not surprisingly, the Blackwood Brothers included this hymn on five of their albums from 1975 through 2018. The song begins with a pondering mood, then quickens with confident assurance as each stanza unpacks the gospel message. Finally it explodes into rising expectancy for Jesus' exultant return. Are you unsure about things in your life right now, or are you at peace with them? Whatever the situation, think of Jesus' sacrifice for you, and stop to thank and praise him. Jesus promises he will return when "faith shall be sight," and he will gather his children to himself forever.

Heavenly Father, I struggle sometimes, wondering what the future holds. Then I remember how you have redeemed me through Jesus. Praise God, "it is well with my soul!"

MARY SAID, "MY SOUL DOTH MAGNIFY THE LORD, AND MY SPIRIT HATH REJOICED IN GOD MY SAVIOUR."
LUKE 1:46-47, KJV

Horatio Spafford, a Chicago lawyer, was a friend of D. L. Moody. In 1873, Spafford's family departed for a European vacation while Spafford attended to urgent business. Halfway across the Atlantic, their ship sank, and his four daughters perished. During his voyage to reunite with his wife, Spafford wrote the lyrics to this hymn.

The Lighthouse

One of the most popular songs in Southern Gospel, "The Lighthouse" was written in 1970 by then teenager Ronny Hinson. Although many groups have covered this tune, The Original Hinsons' heartfelt version—with brothers Ronny, Kenny, Larry, and sister Yvonne—made it a hit. Ironically, Ronny had never seen an actual lighthouse before writing the song. When he finally gazed at one in person, the connection amazed him. Jesus is our Lighthouse, who shines in the dark storms of life. When all seems lost, he is still there. Is Jesus your guiding beacon? Don't navigate life without him. Call on him, and he will save you.

Lord Jesus, I recall your faithfulness when I was drifting in dangerous waters, unable to see the shore. How thankful I am that you will always shine your light and lead me home.

THE PEOPLE WHO SAT IN DARKNESS HAVE SEEN A GREAT LIGHT. AND FOR THOSE WHO LIVED IN THE LAND WHERE DEATH CASTS ITS SHADOW, A LIGHT HAS SHINED.

MATTHEW 4:16

The Hinson family has enjoyed success in Southern Gospel for more than five decades. At first, the siblings' repertoire consisted of gospel covers. When they needed new material for an important concert, Ronny excused himself, only to return a few minutes later with the words of "The Lighthouse" written on a piece of toilet paper.

A light
has
shined

Purchase of God

Blessed Assurance

At the Speer Family's Diamond Jubilee, Brock Speer introduced this family favorite by saying, "Can't beat the old hymns." There may not be another Southern Gospel song that captures so well the sheer ecstasy of finding new life in Christ. But for all the mountaintop emotion of the tune, there's a line that grounds the song in truth: "This is my story, this is my song." Can you remember when you accepted Jesus into your life? Think about that time. It was a turning point for you because Jesus became your story. What evidence of his presence have you experienced lately?

Lord Jesus, thank you for the story of salvation. I want you to be the protagonist in my life. May I be an effective and compelling witness for you.

THIS IS THE SECRET: CHRIST LIVES IN YOU.
THIS GIVES YOU ASSURANCE OF SHARING HIS GLORY.
COLOSSIANS 1:27

Hymn writer Fanny Crosby was visiting her friend Phoebe Knapp when Knapp played Crosby a new melody she had written. "What do you think the song says?" she asked Crosby. There was no hesitation in Crosby's answer: "Blessed assurance. Jesus is mine." The first line of the song was finished.

There Is a Fountain

To people who are not followers of Jesus, the idea of a song about a "fountain filled with blood" sounds bizarre. But to his followers, Jesus' shed blood symbolizes freedom—freedom from bondage to compulsions and addictions and wrong patterns of behavior. The Cross has saved us from slavery to sin. The blood symbolizes baptism of the heart and soul, the washing away of failures and sins—all to make us right with God. Let the Norton Hall Band lead you in "There Is a Fountain," and don't hold back your tears. You know how precious his blood is to you.

Father God, thank you for sending your Son, Jesus, to sacrifice his lifeblood for me. His death was a merciful and incomprehensible gift that restored my relationship with you. I am deeply grateful.

GOD PAID A RANSOM TO SAVE YOU FROM THE EMPTY LIFE
YOU INHERITED. . . . IT WAS NOT PAID WITH MERE GOLD OR
SILVER. . . . IT WAS THE PRECIOUS BLOOD OF CHRIST,
THE SINLESS, SPOTLESS LAMB OF GOD.

1 PETER 1:18-19

Poet and hymn writer William Cowper was a committed evangelical Christian who was a good friend of John Newton, the writer of "Amazing Grace." Cowper struggled much of his life with mental health issues. This hymn was written after one of his first bouts with depression. Hopefully his own words gave him solace.

Lose
all their
guilty
stains

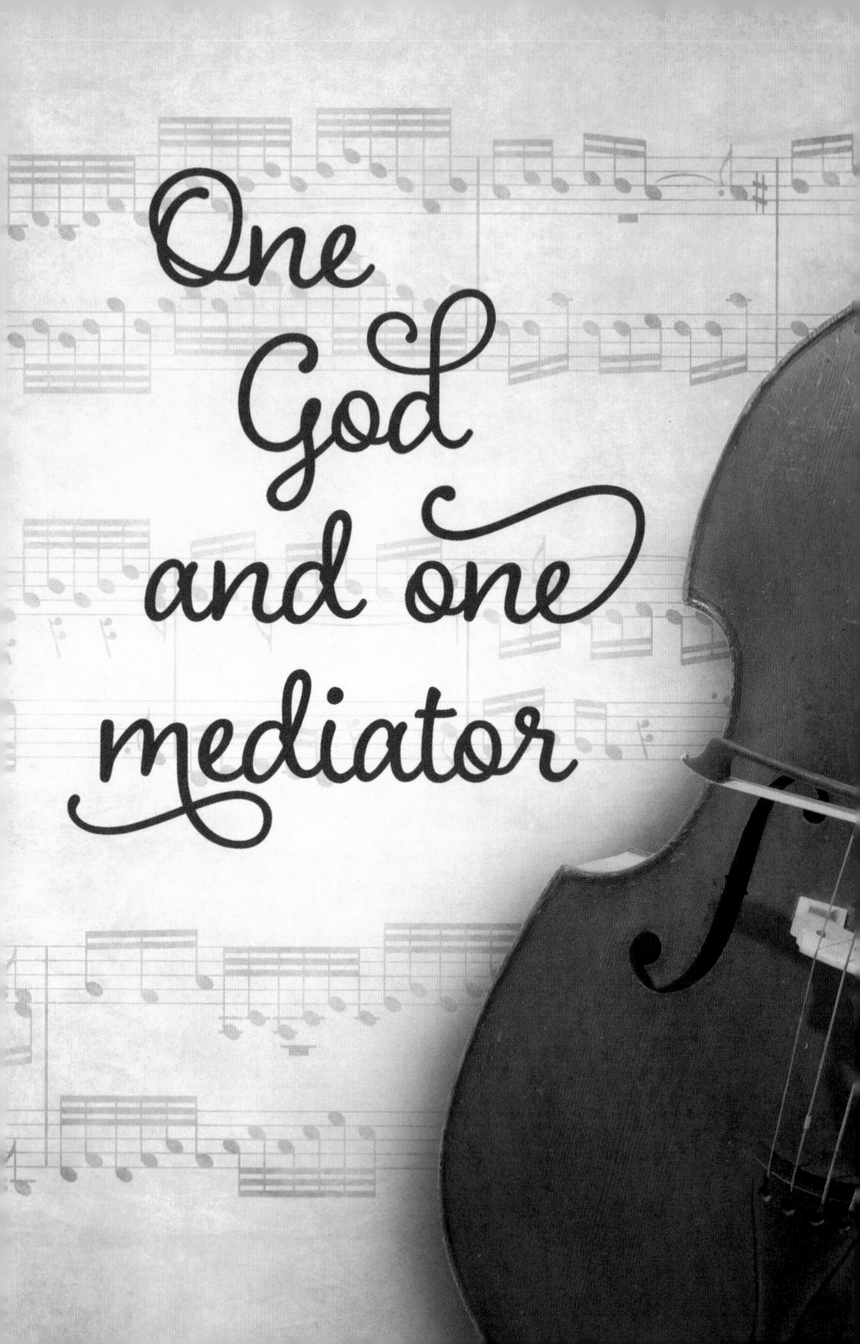
One God and one mediator

I'll Meet You in the Morning

Reunions on earth are sweet, allowing you to catch up with people who've been part of your life. Yet, like the theme of this song, the best reunions of all take place in heaven. Albert Brumley's lyrics transport us to the heavenly realm, where close friends and family who were followers of Jesus await our arrival. But what about someone you love who doesn't believe in Jesus? Perhaps this song is a nudge for you to share the gospel message with them, even if you already have in the past. Ask God to communicate his love for them through you.

Dear God, you know those who are on my mind right now. I pray for the right circumstance to talk to them about you. Please open their hearts and give me the right words to say.

THERE IS ONE GOD, AND ONE MEDIATOR BETWEEN GOD AND MEN, THE MAN CHRIST JESUS; WHO GAVE HIMSELF A RANSOM FOR ALL.

1 TIMOTHY 2:5-6, KJV

Albert Brumley wrote this song in 1936, while he was still on staff at the Hartford Music Company. Eight years later, he opened Albert E. Brumley & Sons Music in Powell, Missouri, and began publishing songbooks. In 1968, Brumley started what has become the Brumley Gospel Sing, a four-day gospel music festival.

'Til the Storm Passes By

Are you feeling anxious, worried, maybe even panicked about things that seem reeling out of control? Oftentimes, life is overwhelming, and you want God to answer your cry. Let the lyrics of this song assure you that despite the deafening thunder of your trials, God hears your desperate plea, and he will keep you safe. As Jesus' disciples found out, he has power even over raging winds and pounding waves—as well as the circumstances of each person's life. You don't need to wake Jesus up to get his attention; you just need to fully trust in him.

Jesus, I don't know whether I can survive the turbulent situations in my life right now. It feels as though I might drown. Please, Lord, rescue me.

SUDDENLY, A FIERCE STORM STRUCK THE LAKE. . . . BUT JESUS WAS SLEEPING. THE DISCIPLES WENT AND WOKE HIM UP, SHOUTING, "LORD, SAVE US! WE'RE GOING TO DROWN!". . . THEN [JESUS] GOT UP AND REBUKED THE WIND AND WAVES, AND SUDDENLY THERE WAS A GREAT CALM. THE DISCIPLES WERE AMAZED. "WHO IS THIS MAN?" THEY ASKED. "EVEN THE WINDS AND WAVES OBEY HIM!"

MATTHEW 8:24-27

Baritone Mosie Lister sang with The Sunny South Quartet, The Melody Masters, and The Statesmen before transitioning to full-time songwriting. "'Til the Storm Passes By" was completed in 1958. Lister was inducted into the Gospel Music Hall of Fame in 1976 and the Southern Gospel Music Association Hall of Fame in 1997.

All to
Chim
I owe

Jesus Paid It All

In the first stanza of this song, much beloved by Southern Gospel groups, songwriter Elvina Hall shares the words Jesus has spoken to her heart. His advice to "watch and pray" and find in him "thine all in all" speaks to his accessibility and trustworthiness. When you feel stressed, even before you start your day, the Savior who knows your heart better than anyone else is there for you. In him, you are given the strength to persevere and the courage to overcome whatever you are facing. You are empowered by the Holy Spirit—God himself—who "prays for us" (Romans 8:26).

Lord Jesus, thank you for saving me from the life I had been leading and delivering me from the consequences of my sin. I'm forever grateful that now I can stand blameless before you.

THOUGH YOUR SINS BE AS SCARLET, THEY SHALL BE AS WHITE AS SNOW; THOUGH THEY BE RED LIKE CRIMSON, THEY SHALL BE AS WOOL.

ISAIAH 1:18, KJV

One Sunday in 1865, hymn writer Elvina Hall was in church when she started jotting down thoughts about Jesus inside a hymnal. After the service, she showed the lyrics to her pastor. By "coincidence" the organist of the church, John Grape, had given the pastor a new tune. The lyrics and tune fit perfectly.

Beyond the Sunset

On a summer night in 1936 in Winona Lake, Indiana, Virgil Brock and his wife, Blanche, were having dinner with Horace and Grace Burr. Watching the sunset's vivid colors, Horace excitedly commented on the spectacular display. Virgil, knowing that Horace was blind, asked how he could possibly see it. Horace replied, "Why, I can see beyond the sunset." This inspired Virgil to sit down at the piano and write music and a chorus to accompany A. K. Rowswell's 1935 poem, "Should You Go First." "Beyond the Sunset" reminds us that those who believe in Jesus will spend a glorious eternity with him.

Lord God, thank you for your promise of abundant life.
May your light shine through me while I'm still on earth,
waiting to reunite with my loved ones in heaven.

NOW WE SEE THROUGH A GLASS, DARKLY; BUT THEN FACE TO FACE: NOW I KNOW IN PART; BUT THEN SHALL I KNOW EVEN AS ALSO I AM KNOWN.

1 CORINTHIANS 13:12, KJV

Virgil Brock was a minister, and Blanche was a classically trained musician. "Beyond the Sunset" was featured in a vaudeville act, recorded by Hank Williams in 1950, and popularized by Jo Stafford and Gordon MacRae in 1962. The lyrics for the entire song are engraved between Virgil's and Blanche's gravestones.

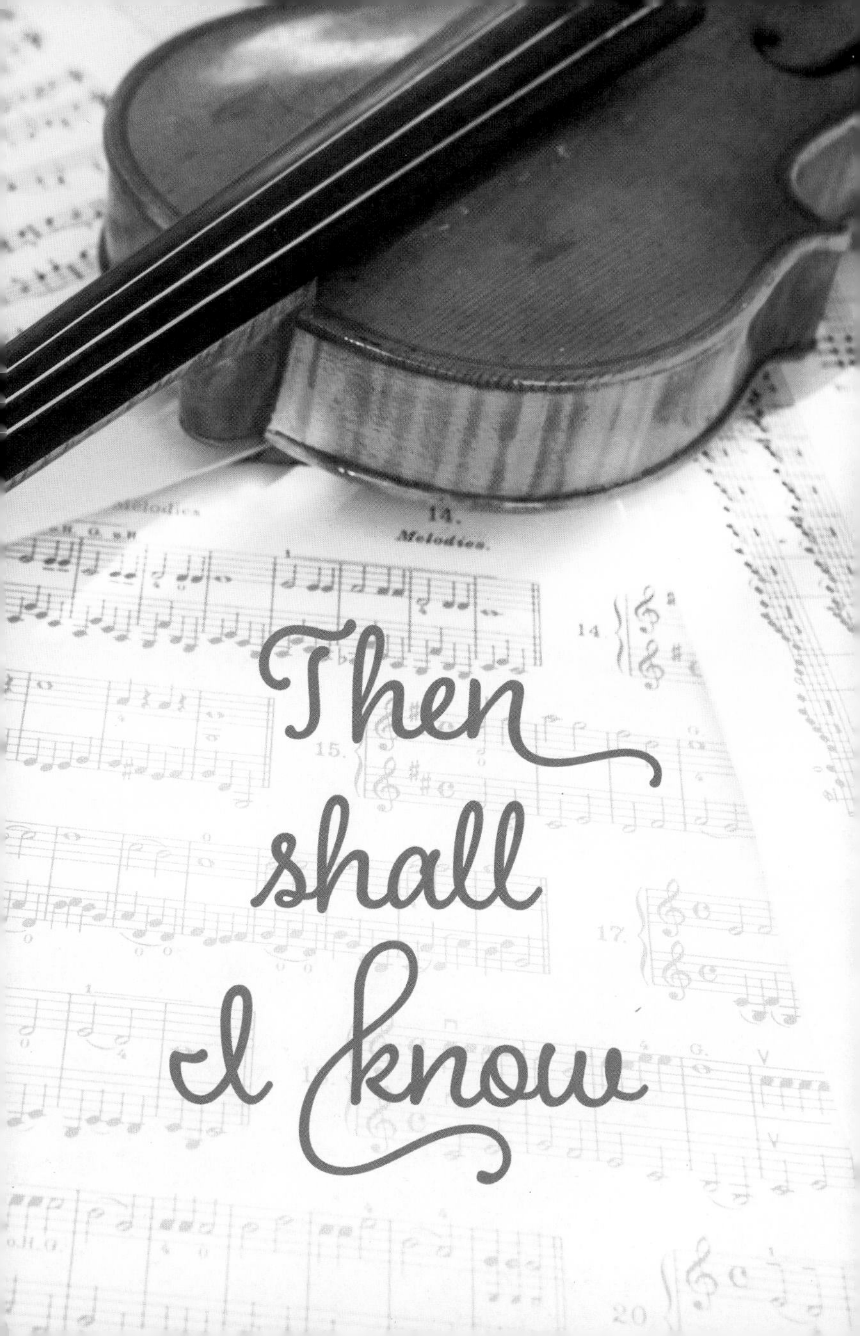

Then shall I know

I Know Who Holds Tomorrow

It's easy to get so wrapped up in our problems and in projecting what calamity might happen tomorrow that our prayer times turn into frettin' times. Take some time to reread Jesus' Sermon on the Mount in the book of Matthew. About midway through (6:34), Jesus offers this advice with a promise: *Don't get worked up about tomorrow, because God will help you with whatever hard things come up.* Planning for the future is a good habit, but as this song so wonderfully reminds us, worrying about the future is a waste of time. Focus on Jesus now, and he will care for you.

> *Lord Jesus, I admit I'm a worrier. When I fixate on problems instead*
> *of focusing on you, I get distraught. Thank you for knowing*
> *what my tomorrow will bring and meeting my needs.*

DON'T WORRY ABOUT TOMORROW, FOR TOMORROW WILL BRING ITS OWN
WORRIES. TODAY'S TROUBLE IS ENOUGH FOR TODAY.

MATTHEW 6:34

Ira Stanphill was at his lowest point after his first wife, Zelda, turned her back on him and God. Some people thought Ira should leave the ministry after she divorced him, but when God's Spirit impressed this song on the evangelist's heart, he had peace to continue. Its message still provides hope to people today.

Goodbye, World, Goodbye

Mosie Lister's song "Goodbye, World, Goodbye" focuses on happy farewells—telling worldly troubles to take a hike. Right now, step back and let the apostle Paul's words to "not lose heart" encourage you. Life takes its toll, sure, but inwardly, God is renewing you each day. When you fix your eyes upon Jesus, you see what is important and lasting. It becomes clear that all your troubles are temporary. One day you will say bye-bye to the blues forever. In the meantime, you can thank God for the good life you have in him.

Father God, please keep me from being distracted by insignificant matters, and help me to focus on Jesus and all that you've given me instead.

WE DO NOT LOSE HEART. THOUGH OUTWARDLY WE ARE WASTING AWAY, YET INWARDLY WE ARE BEING RENEWED DAY BY DAY. FOR OUR LIGHT AND MOMENTARY TROUBLES ARE ACHIEVING FOR US AN ETERNAL GLORY THAT FAR OUTWEIGHS THEM ALL. SO WE FIX OUR EYES NOT ON WHAT IS SEEN, BUT ON WHAT IS UNSEEN, SINCE WHAT IS SEEN IS TEMPORARY, BUT WHAT IS UNSEEN IS ETERNAL.

2 CORINTHIANS 4:16-18, NIV

Mosie Lister's long career as a songwriter began in earnest after he left The Statesmen Quartet as a singer and began writing for them. He was considered the most influential gospel songwriter in the 1950s, with nearly every gospel group including a Lister song in their sets.

Renewed day by day

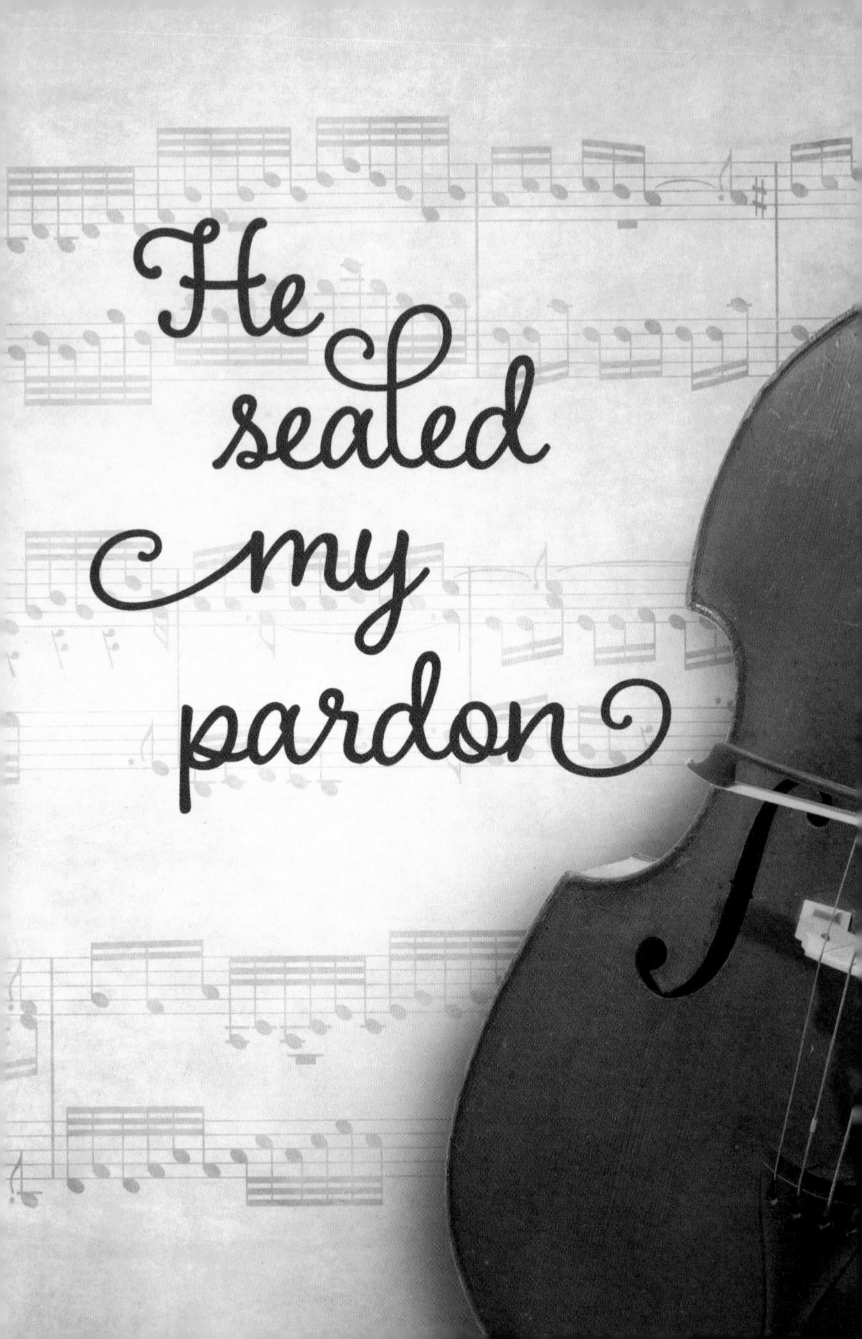
He sealed my pardon

I Will Sing of My Redeemer

We don't often use the word *redeem* these days. The online definitions at *Merriam-Webster* contain words such as *free*, *release*, *clear*, *restore*. All those actions hold true for those who believe in and follow Jesus, the Redeemer. He has freed them from sin, released them from its consequences, cleared them from blame, and restored them to the Father. Isn't that worth praise right now? Even if your walk with God has taken some detours and you've gotten off track, circle back to this truth, and grasp it tightly. Jesus paid the price for your sins and mine.

Lord Jesus, I am one with the Father because of what you did for me.
I can't keep that to myself. Help me to acknowledge your great gift
with song and testimony.

WE SHOULD LIVE SOBERLY, RIGHTEOUSLY, AND GODLY, IN THIS PRESENT
WORLD; LOOKING FOR THAT BLESSED HOPE, AND THE GLORIOUS APPEARING
OF THE GREAT GOD AND OUR SAVIOUR JESUS CHRIST; WHO GAVE HIMSELF
FOR US, THAT HE MIGHT REDEEM US FROM ALL INIQUITY.

TITUS 2:12-14, KJV

In late December 1876, evangelist D. W. Whittle's song leader, Philip Bliss, along with Bliss's wife, were traveling to Chicago for services at Dwight L. Moody's Tabernacle. Enroute, a bridge collapsed, and their train fell into the freezing water below. The couple did not survive. The text of this hymn was found in Bliss's trunk.

Through It All

Do you praise God only when things are going well? Or do you thank him in the middle of the hard times too? Often it's during our most challenging days—when we are at the end of our ropes—that our helplessness is what helps us. We plead with God to show up. And even as we implore him, we are learning to trust him more deeply. Do you feel like you're going "through it all"? Ask God to draw closer. Thank him and praise him, not only for what he has done but also for what he *will* do.

Dear God, life's difficulties take everything out of me and make me fearful. When I'm faced with more than I can endure, please fill me with your power and confidence.

COUNT IT ALL JOY, MY BROTHERS, WHEN YOU MEET TRIALS
OF VARIOUS KINDS, FOR YOU KNOW THAT THE TESTING OF YOUR FAITH
PRODUCES STEADFASTNESS.

JAMES 1:2-3, ESV

"Through It All," written by Andraé Crouch in 1971, came out of personal grief, after his parents and brother had died within a two-year span. At one of his lowest points, Crouch sensed God asking him for praise, not laments. Crouch reluctantly obeyed. The Lord's joy replaced his sorrow and became his musical inspiration.

Promises
that
cannot
fail

Standing on the Promises

If you've experienced an old-fashioned camp meeting, you know the thrill of a crowd heartily singing old gospel tunes. At some point, the pianist might play the familiar introduction to this song while the leader says, "You can't stay seated for this next one!" You may already know by heart the words of this longtime favorite, but look again at this line in the final stanza: "Listening every moment to the Spirit's call." Sometimes we let our faith get lazy, and we stop paying attention. What about you? Are you listening to God's voice and following the Holy Spirit's leading in your life?

Father God, forgive me for letting my convictions slide, for not representing you well, and for simply not being in sync with you. Help me to stay grounded in your Word and fortified by your promises.

LET THE HOLY SPIRIT GUIDE YOUR LIVES. THEN YOU WON'T BE DOING WHAT YOUR SINFUL NATURE CRAVES.

GALATIANS 5:16

Russell Kelso Carter was a remarkable man: athlete, coach, teacher, minister, physician, and hymn writer. Near the age of thirty, he was diagnosed with a life-threatening heart condition and recommitted himself to God's plans for his life. Scripture suddenly became more real to him. He lived another forty-nine years.

His Eye Is on the Sparrow

Maybe you've decided God is too busy to take an interest in you. After all, he's in heaven, attending to principalities and powers. How could he have time for you? But if God were really disengaged, he wouldn't have sent Jesus to walk among us, to die for us, to save us. He wouldn't have given us his Spirit to whisper his guidance. God, who made the entire universe, is aware of every aspect of his creation—from distant galaxies to majestic mountains to the tiniest sparrow. Yet of all his wonders, you are the most precious to him. That's the beauty of the gospel story.

Father God, I admit I've been the one who has been distant from you.
Please close the gap with your love by helping me draw close to you.

NOT A SINGLE SPARROW CAN FALL TO THE GROUND WITHOUT YOUR FATHER KNOWING IT. AND THE VERY HAIRS ON YOUR HEAD ARE ALL NUMBERED. SO DON'T BE AFRAID; YOU ARE MORE VALUABLE TO GOD THAN A WHOLE FLOCK OF SPARROWS.

MATTHEW 10:29-31

One day in 1905, Civilla and Walter Martin were visiting new friends. Mrs. Doolittle was bedridden, and her husband was in a wheelchair. When Walter asked why they still seemed happy, Mrs. Doolittle said, "His eye is on the sparrow, and I know he watches me." That simple truth inspired Civilla to pen the words to this memorable song.

I know
he watches
me
14.
Melodies.

The
delightful
bride
of God

Sweet Beulah Land

If you've never heard the phrase "Beulah Land," you might wonder whether it's another name for heaven. In a sense, it is, and Squire Parsons makes that connection in his lyrics. The Hebrew word *Beulah* means "married," and it appears only once in the Bible. Isaiah 62:4 says that Jerusalem will no longer be forsaken but will be called "Beulah" (NIV). "Beulah Land," then, is the delightful Bride of God, an honored place in his eyes. What is your standing with God? Are you in a forsaken, desolate place because of disobedience? Or are you in a place of God's pleasure?

Father God, I confess and repent of my sins. I long to find your
favor once again. I want to be your joy and pleasure.
Take me, Lord, into Beulah Land with you.

IN MY DISTRESS I CRIED OUT TO THE LORD; YES, I PRAYED TO MY GOD FOR HELP.
HE HEARD ME FROM HIS SANCTUARY; MY CRY TO HIM REACHED HIS EARS. . . .
HE LED ME TO A PLACE OF SAFETY; HE RESCUED ME BECAUSE HE DELIGHTS IN ME.

PSALM 18:6, 19

Southern Gospel musician Squire Parsons was introduced to music with shape note singing. He wrote his signature song in 1973 and recorded it in 1979. In 1981, The Kingsmen Quartet's recording of the song became the number one Southern Gospel single and received the Singing News Fan Award for Song of the Year.

I Heard the Voice of Jesus Say

Perhaps you're beyond tired, worn out from a lifetime of work and responsibilities and the burdens that have come with them. Certain words of this beautiful song—*weary*, *worn*, and *sad*—might echo your feelings today. Yet the song also counters those words with three life-giving blessings that Jesus offers: *rest*, *living water*, and *light*. Whatever you're going through right now, he invites you into his presence in a fresh way. Open your heart as you come to him and rest; drink from his words in the Bible and be refreshed. Know that Jesus is your light in this very dark world.

Lord Jesus, I am exhausted from fighting endless evil in this world. Refresh me with your living water. Shine your light on the path ahead of me.

COME UNTO ME, ALL YE THAT LABOUR AND ARE HEAVY LADEN,
AND I WILL GIVE YOU REST.
MATTHEW 11:28, KJV

Horatius Bonar came from a long line of Scottish ministers. He, too, became a pastor, as well as a hymn writer and prolific author. He traveled to Egypt and Palestine to gain factual background for his sermons and writings. His hymns came to him spontaneously, often during a railroad journey.

I will give you rest

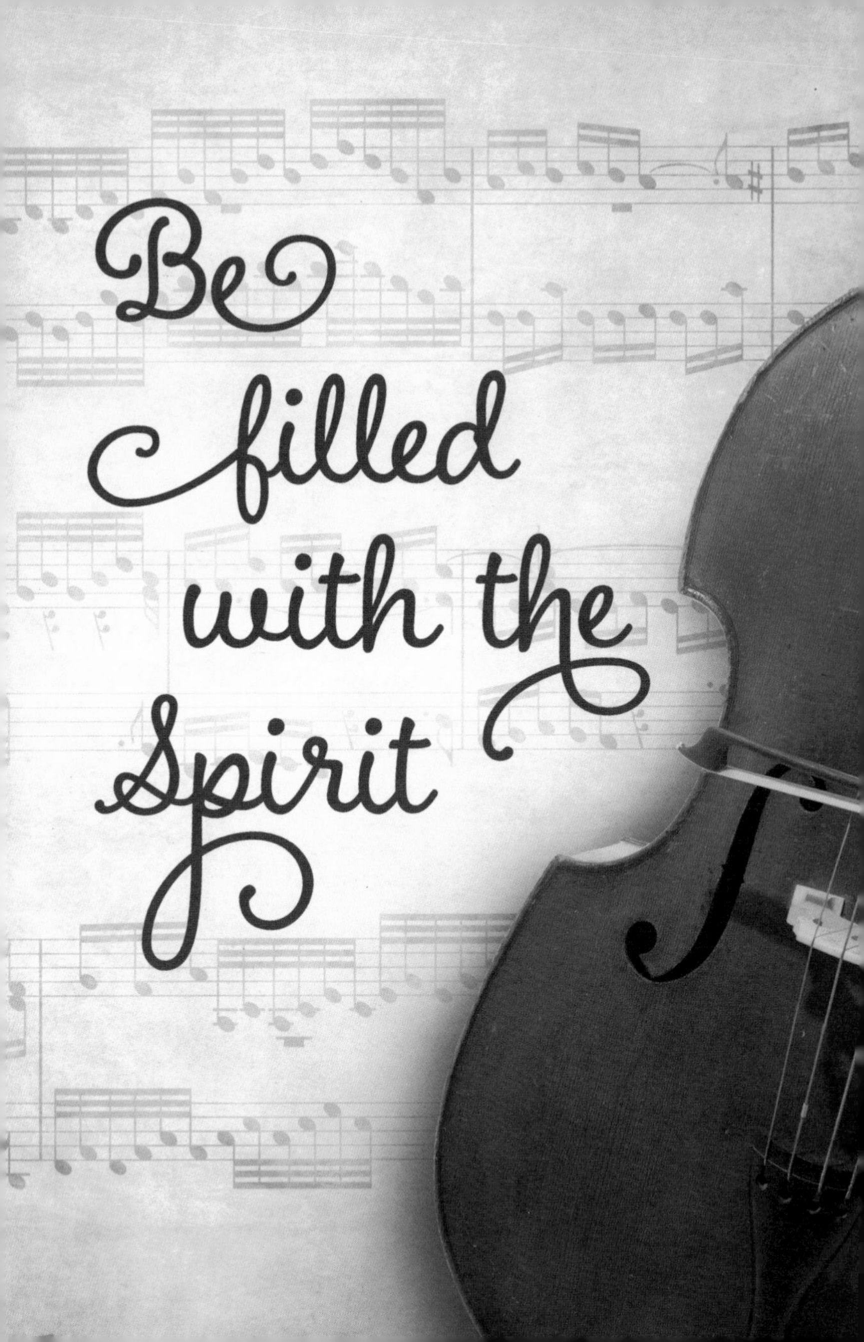
Be filled with the Spirit

The Old Country Church

Did you grow up in a small country church? The building might not have been mighty in size, but what happened inside likely impacted your life forever. A fervent preacher would deliver a solid message on Sunday morning, and that evening, everyone would come ready to sing. Some of the lyrics from those oft-requested tunes are repeated in "The Old Country Church," J. D. Sumner's nostalgic trip back to his own spiritual home. Maybe you have fond memories of an inspirational moment in your past that reminds you of a closer walk with the Lord. Think of someone who could benefit from hearing your story.

Dear God, the close fellowship and joyful praise reflected in this song warm my heart. Would you open up opportunities for me to experience this kind of worship?

BE FILLED WITH THE SPIRIT; SPEAKING TO YOURSELVES IN PSALMS AND HYMNS AND SPIRITUAL SONGS, SINGING AND MAKING MELODY IN YOUR HEART TO THE LORD.

EPHESIANS 5:18-19, KJV

John Daniel Sumner was a prolific songwriter and singer through much of the last century. He was a member of the Blackwood Brothers and other gospel quartets, including his own group, J. D. Sumner and the Stamps. For eighteen years, Sumner held the Guinness World Record for singing the lowest recorded bass note.

Mansion over the Hilltop

The hope of heaven is a theme that many gospel songwriters have put into words. You can't stop smiling about the prospect when you're singing this song, as Jeanne Johnson did at a Gaither Homecoming, or as Eva Mae and Mylon LeFevre did at another Homecoming, with the songwriter, Ira Stanphill, joining them. Since the Bible doesn't give us a lot of specific details about heaven, we don't know exactly what it's like, but we *do* know that when we are "away from these earthly bodies . . . then we will be at home with the Lord" (2 Corinthians 5:7-8). Hallelujah!

Father God, some days I think it would be easier to be in heaven. For now, when I'm anxious, please fill my mind with visions of our eternal home.

———————————

LET NOT YOUR HEART BE TROUBLED: YE BELIEVE IN GOD, BELIEVE ALSO IN ME.
IN MY FATHER'S HOUSE ARE MANY MANSIONS: IF IT WERE NOT SO,
I WOULD HAVE TOLD YOU. I GO TO PREPARE A PLACE FOR YOU.

JOHN 14:1-2, KJV

Musician and evangelist Ira F. Stanphill wrote "Mansion over the Hilltop" in 1949. Recordings of the song sold more than two million copies, with artists such as Elvis and well-known quartets including it on gospel albums. Stanphill wrote more than 550 songs and in 1981 was inducted into the Gospel Music Hall of Fame.

God's
truth
abideth
still

A Mighty Fortress Is Our God

If you think this beloved hymn of the Reformation is only for hundred-voice choirs, listen to the Couriers sing a lively Southern Gospel rendition in three-part harmony. Whichever version you prefer, pay attention to the words, especially these: "And though this world, with devils filled, should threaten to undo us, we will not fear, for God hath willed his truth to triumph through us." Maybe this is especially important to you right now. At a time when the world seems to be caving in, when evil runs rampant and problems keep a-comin', rest assured that the Lord is your rock-solid protector and redeemer.

Father God, I am fearful about what's happening today.
Many people seem to be angry and are acting against your good
laws. I am running to your safety. Keep my faith strong.

I LOVE YOU, LORD; YOU ARE MY STRENGTH. THE LORD IS MY ROCK, MY
FORTRESS, AND MY SAVIOR; MY GOD IS MY ROCK, IN WHOM I FIND PROTECTION.
HE IS MY SHIELD, THE POWER THAT SAVES ME, AND MY PLACE OF SAFETY.

PSALM 18:1-2

German Reformer Martin Luther, one of the most influential figures of Christianity, believed Scripture should be available in the common vernacular, so he translated the original Hebrew and Greek text into German. This hymn has often been called "The Battle Hymn of the Reformation" because it inspired many to take up the cause.

Tell Me the Story of Jesus

"Remember the time when . . ." is a great way to jump-sta hilarious, heart tugging, and often meaningful memories th capture a loved one's character. Similarly, stories about Jesus the Bible help us remember who the Son of God is. John 1:1 say "In the beginning the Word [Jesus] already existed," and verse says that he is "the true light, who gives light to everyone." Ha you shared how Jesus came into your life, what he's done for yo what he means to you? Maybe now is the time to tell that stor God will bring the people who need to hear.

Lord Jesus, thank you for being the center of my story and for
the way you completely changed my life. I praise you for every
chapter that you've written and continue to write.

IN ALL YOUR HISTORY, HAS ANYTHING LIKE THIS HAPPENED BEFORE? TELL YOUR
CHILDREN ABOUT IT IN THE YEARS TO COME, AND LET YOUR CHILDREN TELL
THEIR CHILDREN. PASS THE STORY DOWN FROM GENERATION TO GENERATION.

JOEL 1:2-3

Frances Jane Crosby, also known as Fanny Crosby, is believed to have used as many as two hundred pseudonyms as credits for her songs, with most of those names unknown. That makes the total number of her works difficult to tally, but it is estimated to be anywhere from 5,500 to 9,000.

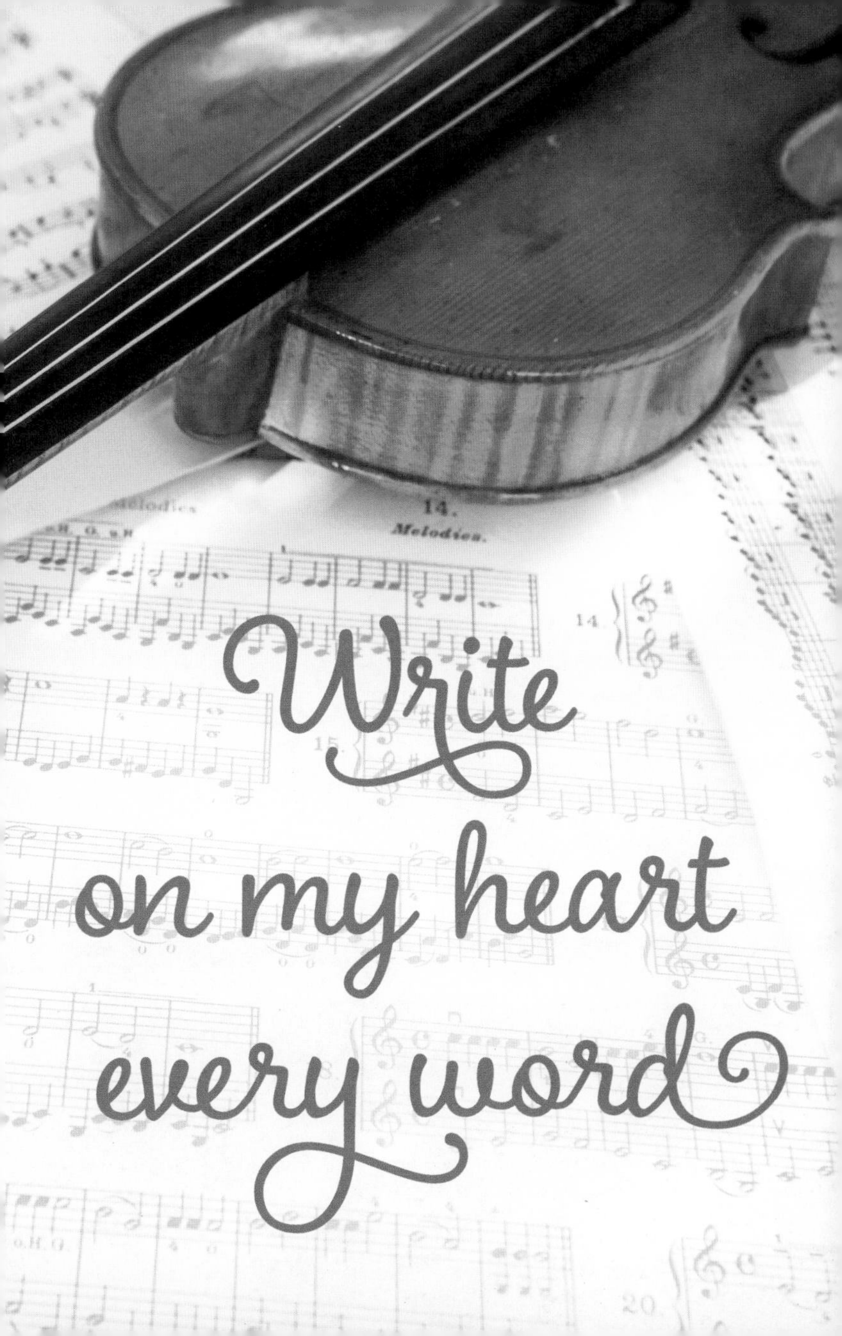
14.
Melodies.
Write
on my heart
every word

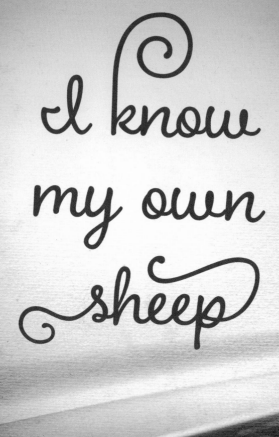

I know my own sheep

Gentle Shepherd

As parents, Gloria and Bill Gaither realized they needed the guidance and wisdom of the Great Shepherd to raise their children, and in reflection, they wrote this song. Are you looking for the Shepherd's help too? Jesus said, "I know my own sheep, and they know me." Jesus calls you by name to come to him, to lean on him, to shelter with him. He offers protection and security, support and care. Share with him your worries, the things that make you wander, the words and situations that scare you. He'll give you his full attention and will offer his assurance and direction.

Lord Jesus, thank you for your watchful eye on me. Even when I stray from your path, you search for me until I am found. You surround me with your love.

I AM THE GOOD SHEPHERD; I KNOW MY OWN SHEEP, AND THEY KNOW ME, JUST AS MY FATHER KNOWS ME AND I KNOW THE FATHER. SO I SACRIFICE MY LIFE FOR THE SHEEP. I HAVE OTHER SHEEP, TOO, THAT ARE NOT IN THIS SHEEPFOLD. I MUST BRING THEM ALSO. THEY WILL LISTEN TO MY VOICE, AND THERE WILL BE ONE FLOCK WITH ONE SHEPHERD.

JOHN 10:14-16

Gloria Gaither's gift for words and Bill's memorable music earned them ASCAP's "Christian Songwriters of the Century" award in 2000. With more than seven hundred songs to their credit, their brands are synonymous with contemporary Christian and gospel music: the Gaither Vocal Band, the Homecoming concert series, Gaither TV, and the Gaither Music Group.